Getting Ready for the New Life

OTHER LUTHERAN VOICES TITLES

See www.lutheranvoices.com

Getting Ready for the New Life
Facing Illness or Death
with the Word and Prayers

Richard F. Bansemer

Augsburg Fortress

Minneapolis

GETTING READY FOR THE NEW LIFE
Facing Illness or Death with the Word and Prayers

Large-quantity purchases or custom editions of these books are available at a discount from the publisher. For more information, contact the sales department at Augsburg Fortress, Publishers, 1-800-328-4648, or write to: Sales Director, Augsburg Fortress, Publishers, P.O. Box 1209, Minneapolis, MN 55440-1209.

Editor: Rochelle Melander

Cover Design: © Koechel Peterson and Associates, Inc., Minneapolis, MN
www.koechelpeterson.com

ISBN 0-8066-4988-7

The paper used in this publication meets the minimum requirements of American National Standard for Information Sciences—Permanence of Paper for Printed Library Materials, ANSI Z329.48-1984.

Manufactured in the U.S.A.

08   07   06   05   04   1   2   3   4   5   6   7   8   9   10

Contents

Introduction

Illness is a great teacher. More convincing than an athlete's achievements, more striking than a perfect physique, illness lets us know, in no uncertain terms, that we are intensely human. When illness comes, the pain cannot be ignored. More importantly, if the illness is serious, mortality cannot be ignored—except by the most skilled in living lives of denial.

Many lessons come through illness. We are taught patience—not through lectures but our own experiences. We need to be patient in order to function. Sometimes illness makes us choose new priorities, real priorities, for the first time in our lives.

Through illness we meet new people and caretakers. Often we can no longer enjoy the modesty of a private body, for it has been poked, probed, cut upon, and washed for us. Our caretakers often know—before we do—how human we really are, and how un-special we are when it comes to our physicality: how we tick and how we are sick.

But illness is more than a teacher. Illness emerges as an event that is historical in our individual lives. We date other events from the time we were hospitalized or from the time when a loved one was ill.

This book of thoughts and prayers has many authors. My own personal experience with illness can hardly be classified as severe, though I've been the recipient of several fine surgical procedures, some of which have been life saving. The illnesses of those I love have had an equally profound effect upon me.

The words that follow belong to many whom I've been privileged to visit while they were ill, or to those who loved them. The ill person is not the only one who struggles when someone is sick. Spouses ache for each other. Parents are overcome with anxiety for their child. Friends suffer when true friends are in trouble. And children, least able to comprehend the devastating consequence of a parent's illness, know intuitively that powers are at work beyond their control. Mom and dad are not gods after all. Or perhaps, they, who once were gods, are now incomprehensibly vulnerable gods.

Nevertheless, illness is most profoundly a personal matter. It is one's very own body in rebellion. No one else can feel the pain or the weakness as acutely as the one who is ill. If it is dying that is being called for, no one else can do it for us.

The reflective Scripture texts were selected as the bridge between the words of this world in the commentary and the prayers to God. The Scripture texts are the Word of God and need to be read even more thoughtfully than the other offerings. Questions for reflection and discussion follow the prayers.

1

Losses

Dealing with loss of health is always a relative matter, since some of us have enjoyed much better health through the years than others of us ever dreamed about having. Talking about diminishing health, however, is common because our prime health comes early on in life, and then the aches and pains of aging begin.

The problem of a having a body is a universally shared phenomenon. In one sense, our bodies are us. Without them we are not here, cannot be seen by another, cannot go anywhere, or do anything. Our bodies are our lives.

On the other hand, our bodies are our problems. They need constant attention, nourishment, and healing. We bathe them, dress them, diet them, and wash them. It raises this profound question: "Why did God give us bodies to dwell in?" Or, if you prefer, "Why did God give us bodies to live through?"

There must be a reason for having a body other than the obvious one of being able to walk, talk, eat, and live as a human being. After all, God could have given us spiritual bodies instead of earthly ones. We could have had bodies like angels and cherubim and seraphim, but God didn't do that. Why?

Having an earthly body, rather than a spiritual body, must serve some purpose for God. The Creator, from the beginning, used physical materials to create the world we know. The Father, in the fullness of time, also sent the Son as a newborn baby, to have the same earth body experience as the rest of us.

While on earth in our body form we get to watch all sorts of bodily transformations. An egg hatches. A bud blooms. "First the blade, then the ear, then the full corn shall appear" (*Lutheran Book of Worship*, 407). We see a lowly caterpillar, then a cocoon, then a flying butterfly with oversized wings of dazzling beauty.

For most of us, it has been a transformation from total helplessness at birth, to growth through childhood, independence in adulthood, and then a return to helplessness near death. The cycle has many more steps, of course, but the beginning and the ending are the same. Why does God want us to have this experience?

It is not in this world alone that God rules, and perhaps it is not on earth alone that God has plans for us. Though we could have been made with spiritual bodies, instead of physical ones, and grown to love and serve God and neighbor through a different sort of life experience, God decided on the physical course for us. For some reason, our physical design is for a life and purpose we do not yet fully understand.

Looking out at the cosmos at night we can see mere pinpricks of light, or the realization that what we call "out there" is God's "here," where physical worlds develop like earth, with wonders more vast than our imaginations can dream. Somehow, God has use for us in this plan for the ages yet to come. Somehow the experience we are now having, in the body, is essential for us to have had in order for us to fully appreciate and be useful to God in the physical world that has yet to be revealed to us. This does not mean that our resurrections are restorations of our physical bodies. It simply means that our resurrections are truly our resurrections—not a new life without a history here. Therefore, every shedding of health we experience upon earth can be viewed not just as dying, though that is part of it, but as transformation into the new creature that God has plans for, forever.

Reflective Text

1 Corinthians 15:35-58

But someone will ask, "How are the dead raised? With what kind of body do they come?" Fool! What you sow does not come to life unless it dies. And as for what you sow, you do not sow the body that is to be, but a bare seed, perhaps of wheat or of some other grain. But God gives it a body as he has chosen, and to each kind of seed its own body. Not all flesh is alike, but there is one flesh for human beings, another for animals, another for birds, and another for fish. There are both heavenly bodies and earthly bodies, but the glory of the heavenly is one thing, and that of the earthly is another. There is one glory of the sun, and another glory of the moon, and another glory of the stars; indeed, star differs from star in glory.

So it is with the resurrection of the dead. What is sown is perishable, what is raised is imperishable. It is sown in dishonor, it is raised in glory. It is sown in weakness, it is raised in power. It is sown a physical body, it is raised a spiritual body. If there is a physical body, there is also a spiritual body. Thus it is written, "The first man, Adam, became a living being"; the last Adam became a life-giving spirit. But it is not the spiritual that is first, but the physical, and then the spiritual. The first man was from the earth, a man of dust; the second man is from heaven. As was the man of dust, so are those who are of the dust; and as is the man of heaven, so are those who are of heaven. Just as we have borne the image of the man of dust, we will also bear the image of the man of heaven.

What I am saying, brothers and sisters, is this: flesh and blood cannot inherit the kingdom of God, nor does the perishable inherit the imperishable. Listen, I will tell you a mystery! We will not all die, but we will all be changed, in a moment, in the twinkling of an eye, at the last trumpet. For the trumpet will sound, and the dead will be raised imperishable, and we will be changed. For this perishable body must put on imperishability, and this mortal body must

put on immortality. When this perishable body puts on imperishability, and this mortal body puts on immortality, then the saying that is written will be fulfilled:
"Death has been swallowed up in victory."
"Where, O death, is your victory?
Where, O death, is your sting?"
The sting of death is sin, and the power of sin is the law. But thanks be to God, who gives us the victory through our Lord Jesus Christ.

Therefore, my beloved, be steadfast, immovable, always excelling in the work of the Lord, because you know that in the Lord your labor is not in vain.

Prayer

I've been taught to count my blessings, Lord, and not complain, but I can't seem to get my losses out of my mind. So many strengths that I took for granted are diminished or gone. I never knew how much you had given me until now. I wonder how much more will be taken away.

There is no possibility of return to full strength. This I know. Much of what I've built my personality around has faded. I don't like the losses. I don't like being reminded how much I've enjoyed good health through the years, and how little I've thanked you for it. Nevertheless, I don't think you want me to feel guilty about enjoying abundant life, past and present. I think you want me to remember it with joy.

So it's not just about learning, is it? You're not teaching me a cruel lesson. It's not about noting how much you've given through the years. It's not an intellectual matter at all. It's not something to make a graph about in order to study the decline.

Rather, I think you are removing idols from my life. You are taking away those things that have been points of physical pride. You take away the glory of youth and replace it with gnarly grace. You tell me to remember everything I can about life in the body because you have yet another plan I cannot see. You want me to imagine life beyond me, beyond my body. You are preparing me for a new life with a new body, fit for living in a new world.

You are from this other world, but you want me to notice you near, notice you here. You want me to rely upon you for the future, but to stay here a while longer. You want me to believe there is a new world coming, and that this life's experiences will matter there. You want me to want you in both worlds. You want to use me in both worlds. Yes, Lord, yes. Whenever you're ready. Amen

---

Reflective Questions

1. What losses in life have been most significant for you? Who helped you to cope with them?
2. Have you ever been able to thank God for a loss, knowing that some sort of gain had been received? If your answer is yes, what happened? If your answer is no, would doing this be helpful to you?
3. Does putting "losses" into the context of eternal life, as described by Paul in 1 Corinthians 15, lessen the pain of losses for you? Why or why not?

2

You Love Me

All of us have trouble with being loved. Trace it back to childhood, look for it in our genes, blame life experiences, or simply believe in original sin, and we have reason enough to have an innate ability to refuse love from a lover. Who wants to be hurt again? Who really feels worthy of it? Who knows how to respond to it?

These same doubts apply to God's love for us. Nothing is harder to accept than God's love. That God the Father might love all of humankind is just fine. That Jesus died for the sins of the whole world is understandable. That the Holy Spirit has been able to put an inspirational chill up our spines, or comfort us on occasion is nice. But God—Father, Son, and Holy Spirit—moving in with me, as one lone individual, well, that appears preposterous, impossible, or even inappropriate to many of us.

Hence, God is put into the crowd where we can watch more safely. Or we can approach God with others through public worship, participating in rousing hymns and stirring prayers.

I know of a pastor who didn't rest enough. He had a fine sense of duty. No one could fault him for not trying. He was a doer until he got sick. Then he told me of his struggles for health, being absent from the congregation for its worship, the loneliness of the night, and the fear of not recovering.

The pastor had a heart full of love for God, but his heart turned against him and attacked him. He required open-heart surgery, not once but twice, though ten years had passed between the attacks. He mused openly with me about the 23rd Psalm where the psalmist says: "He makes me lie down" (Psalm 23:2). This pastor was forced to his bed for rest, because it had never dawned upon him that God, as friend and lover, thinks rest is a good thing, and something that need not be avoided out of a mistaken sense of duty. God illustrated this by his own rest on the seventh day of creation.

But there is more to this quote from the 23rd Psalm that touched this pastor's heart. He understood the psalmist to be saying that sometimes we have to be made to do the right thing. And this is true, and this is what the pastor grasped. But the more amazing word in the phrase "He makes me lie down" is not *makes* but *me*. The whole cosmos may need attending, but God, in infinite love, makes me lie down. Seventeen times in the six verses of Psalm 23 a personal pronoun is used. That's how beloved you are, and why you can say, "I am loved."

Reflective Text
Psalm 23

The Lord is my shepherd, I shall not want.
He makes me lie down in green pastures;
he leads me beside still waters;
he restores my soul.
He leads me in right paths for his name's sake.
Even though I walk through the darkest valley,
I fear no evil;
for you are with me;
your rod and your staff—
they comfort me.
You prepare a table before me
in the presence of my enemies; you anoint my head with oil;
my cup overflows.
Surely goodness and mercy shall follow me
all the days of my life,
and I shall dwell in the house of the Lord
my whole life long.

Prayer

Lord, I'm praying the same old prayer. How many times have you heard me worry about what's next? How many times have you heard me sigh because of your silence?

Am I going to get better or not? I don't know what to plan for, what to hope for, what to ask for. You said to ask for anything in your name and you will do it. In your name, in your name—help me pray in your name.

Of all the thoughts I have about you, Lord, your loving me is the hardest to accept. I get the cosmic scope of things and your work for humankind, but your loving me hardly comes easy. Why would you do such a thing? I'm sick and afraid and hurting and you want to talk about something other than these things.

You love me. I hear the words. You love me. Not what I do or what I say, just me. I can't put this into words. I can't quite believe it. There is nothing about me to love. Still, you love me.

For a moment I believed it. Just now. For a moment you had me near. You touched me. You held me. For a moment I let you do it. For a moment my health didn't matter. You love me. You've come to my bed. Whatever happens, I'm going to be alright. I'm praying in your name. Amen

---

Reflective Questions

1. In prayer, have you let yourself be loved by God? What are some of the prayers or prayer tools that have helped you to do this?

2. Through prayer, have you ever been able to alter a first impulse reaction toward someone who's wronged you? If so, what happened?

3. Are you able to move from talking about God or yourself to talking with God as friend? If your answer is yes, what helped you make this shift?

3

Ready to Die

Almost all of us have known someone who was ready to die. I remember a farmer in a rural area who had terminal cancer. As a young pastor, I went to visit with him and I asked him this insidious question: "How do you feel about having cancer?" I might as well have asked him, "How do you feel about being dead in three months?" He looked right through me and responded without hesitation, "You've got to die of something." And so we do.

I remember visiting with a lady in her late 80s. I marveled at her longevity, which seemed considerable to me at the time. And she, like the farmer above, looked me in the eye and said, "If you are given a long life, you will pay a high price."

Some persons prepare to die by planning their funeral services, complete with lessons, hymns, and other arrangements. Some people will their bodies to science. Some write thank-you notes. Some express confidence, some express fear, and some are matter-of-fact. All of them are saying good-bye to loved ones.

The scheduling of a serious surgical procedure, for any ailment, has a way of waking us up to the reality of "You've got to die of something," or "Have you, through suffering, paid a high-enough price to make you ready to move on?"

This life in the body is the one we know best. Some might argue that this bodily existence is the only life we know at all. Yet we have been told about another time and place—where time is not measured at all and daytime and nighttime do not exist. We have been told about a reunion that follows the resurrection of our bodies. We know these things from the Word of God, and sometimes we know them in our hearts, yet we are reluctant to let go of the life we are living now.

We are able, sometimes, to consider the balance of all the lives we have loved—those who have preceded us in death and those still giving us purpose and joy here. When the balance gets tipped to the other side, when few of our loved ones are still living, some people are able to relax and let go. But the sanctity of life makes others fight for a thousand last breaths, as though some duty is being fulfilled. Maybe it is. I do not know. I do know that many who want to die cannot die, and many who want to live cannot live. The timing is not in our hands.

Reflective Text
Revelation 22:1-7

Then the angel showed me the river of the water of life, bright as crystal, flowing from the throne of God and of the Lamb through the middle of the street of the city. On either side of the river is the tree of life with its twelve kinds of fruit, producing its fruit each month; and the leaves of the tree are for the healing of the nations. Nothing accursed will be found there any more. But the throne of God and of the Lamb will be in it, and his servants will worship him; they will see his face, and his name will be on their foreheads. And there will be no more night; they need no light of lamp or sun, for the Lord God will be their light, and they will reign forever and ever.

And he said to me, "These words are trustworthy and true, for the Lord, the God of the spirits of the prophets, has sent his angel to show his servants what must soon take place."

"See, I am coming soon! Blessed is the one who keeps the words of the prophecy of this book."

Prayer

Lord, my health seems so much out of my control. I'm better off not worrying too much about what's happening. You're the one who said that anxiousness couldn't add a moment to a life. I believe you.

My life is in your hands. I'm glad it is. I've done what I can to prolong it. Tonight I feel very healthy. Like I'm getting stronger. But I know the time will come, and my life will be done.

When you come for me, Lord, may I be as ready as I am right now. Speak softly to me, like lovers do. Lead me to the reunion, Lord, and comfort those who follow. Amen

---

Reflective Questions

1. What does it mean to you to be "ready to die?"
2. If God has "The Whole World in His Hands," this certainly includes you, too. What does this mean for you?
3. God has come in Christ and will return, as indicated in Revelation 22:7: "See, I am coming soon!" Does this bring dread, joy, or some other reaction for you? Why?

4

Tending

People who tend to the needs of the ill often do so without knowing what a gift they are giving. Those engaged in professional care, such as nurses and doctors, are able to do so with some detachment, which is necessary to accomplish certain tasks. The family member who tends to their beloved experiences the task at another level altogether.

When a relative or a very close friend is involved in the care, the stakes are much higher. Thoughts of a pending loss and an inevitable good-bye weigh heavily. The strengths of former years seem distant, and the future is inconceivably painful. These thoughts are not the caregiver's alone. They belong to the one who is seriously ill, too.

Weakness is a powerful magnet. Some are drawn to it out of a sense of empathy, while others are repulsed by it, as though the growing weakness of the beloved makes love hopeless and impractical. But true love is always impractical. The wise understand that the current situation is true reality, and that this experience is filled with opportunities for the kind of hope that expects a future, if not here, then elsewhere.

The first time I ever saw a man massage another man was in the sick room of a stranger dying of cancer. My parishioner had invited me to come along to meet his dying friend and to share a prayer. The dying one was lying low in the bed, but the tender caressing of his frail body by his friend was beauty alive. There were shared smiles and there were sighs of delight, because of the touch of this friend who had come to visit.

The gift of caring is a pearl of great price. It can be learned. The first time we held the hand of another toward whom we felt affection was probably awkward, too. But that simple act, that light touch, communicated a love that words could not convey.

So many of the healing miracles of Jesus involved touch—the leper, the blind man, the slave of the high priest who lost an ear at the arrest of Jesus. Jesus touched and healed them all. A woman touched his garment, Jesus felt the power go out of him, and she was healed. Jesus even touched the bier of a dead man, and the man rose.

Tending involves touching by fingers, voice, tears, hugs, and prayers. Power leaves us when we do it, but it does not make us weaker. It makes us related to one another as true kin. We become a trilogy of folk—the sick, the caregiver, and the ultimate Healer of All Ills. Tending makes the other know that love always prevails, in this world and the next.

Reflective Text
Mark 5:21-43

When Jesus had crossed again in the boat to the other side, a great crowd gathered around him; and he was by the sea. Then one of the leaders of the synagogue named Jairus came and, when he saw him, fell at his feet and begged him repeatedly, "My little daughter is at the point of death. Come and lay your hands on her, so that she may be made well, and live." So he went with him.

And a large crowd followed him and pressed in on him. Now there was a woman who had been suffering from hemorrhages for twelve years. She had endured much under many physicians, and had spent all that she had; and she was no better, but rather grew worse. She had heard about Jesus, and came up behind him in the crowd and touched his cloak, for she said, "If I but touch his clothes, I will be made well." Immediately her hemorrhage stopped; and she felt in her body that she was healed of her disease. Immediately aware that power had gone forth from him, Jesus turned about in the crowd and said, "Who touched my clothes?" And his disciples said to him, "You see the crowd pressing in on you; how can you say, 'Who touched me?'" He looked all around to see who had done it. But the woman, knowing what had happened to her, came in fear and trembling, fell down before him, and told him the whole truth. He said to her, "Daughter, your faith has made you well; go in peace, and be healed of your disease."

While he was still speaking, some people came from the leader's house to say, "Your daughter is dead. Why trouble the teacher any further?" But overhearing what they said, Jesus said to the leader of the synagogue, "Do not fear, only believe." He allowed no one to follow him except Peter, James, and John, the brother of James. When they came to the house of the leader of the synagogue, he saw a commotion, people weeping and wailing loudly. When he had entered, he said to them, "Why do you make a commotion and weep? The child is not dead but sleeping." And they laughed at him. Then he put them all outside, and took the child's father and mother and those who were with him, and went in where the child was. He took her by the hand and said to her, "Talitha cum," which means, "Little girl, get up!" And immediately the girl got up and began to walk about (she was twelve years of age). At this they were overcome with amazement. He strictly ordered them that no one should know this, and told them to give her something to eat.

Prayer

Lord Jesus Christ, Great Physician, how I wish I had your words and touch. I would touch and speak and heal, just like you did, and make my loved one well.

The circumstances, Lord, are very difficult for us. We can hardly bear to see the other's pain. We feel so helpless. How will we find grace in these slow-moving days? We feel pain. Both of us are hurting for the other.

Lord, give us the words that will lessen our pain. Give me a caressing touch that communicates a loving presence. Give us patience for this ordeal.

I am so grateful that my dear one will not have to do this for me. I am honored, Lord, that you have chosen me to do this tending. Deliver us from this suffering, and may we forever be grateful for every moment of love that is yet to be shared. Amen

---

Reflective Questions

1. Have you been touched in a healing way? By whom? In what way was it an incarnation of Christ?
2. How many ways can you think of to touch another lovingly?
3. Jesus said, "My grace is sufficient for you, for power is made perfect in weakness" (2 Corinthians 12:9). Does this mean that our love is most powerful when we are powerless to prevail?

5

Purpose

When an active person becomes disabled, many questions emerge. A primary question is, "What's the purpose of my life now?"

Somewhere implanted in our minds is the value that life means output, and if we can no longer make that output, we no longer have a reason for being. In many ways this sort of thinking dominates us from childhood until death, and it is the basis of the American work ethic. We've been taught to do our share and 10 percent more. The coach of my son's basketball team did the arithmetic for them: "I want 110 percent from every player." I'm pretty sure my son complied with his coach's demand, and it made me glad. I had taught him well.

People who experience cataclysmic illness and survive with grace are marvels of humanity. The ability to achieve a 110 percent output for them is a long-ago memory, and one they smile about now.

A pastor recently told me about a member of his parish who, over a period of six years, became a quadriplegic. She had been one of his most active members, and now she was bedfast. For years he just visited her and marveled, as we sometimes do, over persons who are able to make the best of a bad situation. She had made the passage from a full life of purpose to an apparently lesser life of being waited upon.

One day the pastor gained his courage and asked her, "How do you manage to be so cheerful when I visit, never complaining or pining about the days when you were able to be the most active person in the parish?" She smiled and said, "I'm glad you asked. It took you a long time, but I knew you would eventually ask."

She continued, "I have a confession to make to you, Pastor. All that work I did years ago wasn't really for others. I did it for me. It made me proud, and it's who I thought I was. Now I can't do anything except talk. I can't even go and visit someone. Everyone who wants to be around me for a while has to come here. And people do. I've become a kind of viaduct for them. I'm a bridge over their harried lives. Though I don't like this situation, they know that I'm at peace. But they do not know how I can have joys surpassing their own. They're doing what I was doing. With a wary eye they're watching to see if my present kind of life is a real life. I can assure you it is. Surprises walk into my life every day—like you coming by to ask me an important question, not just a busy question. But most important of all, I have the perfect excuse to give up the hopeless quest for meaning through busyness. It just isn't there. It's a much quieter and gentler matter. It's happening, you know, right here, right now. This conversation and communication between us could never have happened years ago. I wouldn't have had time to listen. You wouldn't have thought I had much to say. Now, this is all that I can be, and God seems to be quite satisfied with it. So, why shouldn't I?"

If our purpose is to be anything other than self-gratification, it needs to have a point of reference away from us. When I listen to the witness of the women above, what strikes me most poignantly is not her courage, though that is very significant. Rather, it is her vocation as a viaduct for persons who wish to rise above the busyness of their rushed, ant-like lives, where there is no real wisdom to all their huff and hurry. Purpose belongs to God alone. It's the will above every will, and the assurance that whatever befalls us will be used by God for a higher purpose, even if we cannot see it now.

Reflective Text

Isaiah 55:6-11

Seek the Lord while he may be found,
call upon him while he is near;
let the wicked forsake their way,
and the unrighteous their thoughts;
let them return to the Lord, that he may have mercy on them,
and to our God, for he will abundantly pardon.
For my thoughts are not your thoughts,
nor are your ways my ways, says the Lord.
For as the heavens are higher than the earth,
so are my ways higher than your ways
and my thoughts than your thoughts.
For as the rain and the snow come down from heaven,
and do not return there until they have watered the earth,
making it bring forth and sprout,
giving seed to the sower and bread to the eater,
so shall my word be that goes out from my mouth;
it shall not return to me empty,
but it shall accomplish that which I purpose,
and succeed in the thing for which I sent it.

Prayer

I've wondered about my purpose, Lord. I've wondered if you've noticed how out-of-sorts I am. I overheard someone say that I am difficult. I know it's true, because I don't know what's coming next. I know enough to have cause to worry.

Lord, I don't think I can be like the brave who make peace with adversity. I'm a fighter. I'm a survivor. I have a will to live and a will to get better. You know I worship quality life.

I have my idol, my very own precious idol: my health at any cost. I can't wait to get better, to have the strength I had before, to walk and run and tire slowly.

I wonder about your purpose for me, Lord. That is a better curiosity. I wonder if I will only go kicking and screaming into my next phase of life. I suppose so. They told me that I kicked and screamed at my baptism, but you claimed me anyway.

Lord, I do love life. I love worshiping you by noticing the beauty of your creation. I love noting the details of your handiwork in this world. I think of you when the morning birds sing, thunder rumbles, and rain falls.

I think of you especially in springtime, when tender sprouts push the wet heavy leafs aside one by one, like some living, miniature bulldozer moving boulders. Such a struggle the sprout has in order to send up stem and leaf to feed the bloom that's still hidden somewhere within.

Lord Jesus, I see what you're doing. I understand the need for struggle and change, though I struggle against it. Have it your way—if it's the only way that makes another season of flowering possible, even for me. Amen

---

Reflective Questions

1. What struggles have you had that were life changing or life strengthening?
2. According to God's holy purposes, and not your own, how is God using you now?
3. Who has served as a bridge of peace over your busy life? In what ways have they ministered to you?

6

The Point

Some people say, "I have no regrets," even at the end of their lives. It can be a glib, defensive statement to a thoughtlessly lived life—a slick way to pretend that I really did it "my way."

If we are to be honest with ourselves, we probably have to admit to having missed the point of being God's person on many occasions, and even now, during suffering, miss it still. Yet I know of no place in Scripture where guilt is heaped upon the faithful sufferer, except in certain lamentations where psalmists take themselves to task or insincere friends give Job false care.

The point of life cannot be intellectually defined. If it were so, perhaps only the greatest of philosophers could die rightly—like Socrates tried to do with his cup of hemlock. The rest of us would be consigned to lesser deaths.

Every man's death and every woman's death is their most profound moment of transition. It is equal to anyone else's dying. It is the one event that no one else can do for us, no matter how many prayers are said or how many people hold our hand. I have to do it. You have to do it. And there is no one living, in the physical sense of living, who can help us do this. All the rest of us have yet to do it.

If I were to ascribe one attribute to Jesus above all others it would have nothing to do with his power, faithfulness, parentage, love of God, or sense of mission, though all these things are important. It is Jesus's kingly kindness that touches me. It is his calling us to be his friends even though he is king. It is Jesus's caring about a dying thief during his own dying that is indescribably compassionate. It is Jesus's caring for his mother during his own dying that makes us understand why we want our own family about us when we leave this world. It is Jesus's caring about all the guilt we might carry for his death on our behalf that makes him exclaim during his own dying, "Father, forgive them; they do not know . . . " (Luke 23:34).

What we don't know, and can hardly begin to fathom, is the depth of the Father's love for us—a love so deep that the Father thought that the death of our king, Jesus Christ, was not too great a price to pay in order to accomplish all things for our salvation. It's not just kindness that's the point. It is Jesus's divine and human kingly kindness, of such power than no other mortal can ever duplicate it. Lots of kind people die every day, and when our time comes we will be one of them. Only Christ's death has salvation inherent within it for all of us. So then, what is left to carry us through? What can we look for, and what can we do in our dying?

From those who come to visit with us, we can look for their kindness. It is far more helpful than their wisdom.

From ourselves, as we die, we can expect an unusual strength to be kind. It will come. It is as sure as God, because God gives it. It is the power to say some things to those we love that we never had the courage to say before. And if the voice no longer transports the message because of its failing, love is still conveyed.

From God we can expect the ultimate kindness, because the Son has been where we are when our dying time comes. The Son, reflective of the Father, is kindness and kingliness through and through. The point has nothing to do with our courage at the time of our dying. God's grace, God's kindness, and our own, is made perfect in weakness—abject weakness—not a little weakness, but total weakness. Weakness is good enough for God, when it's all we have left. Then God's grace is made perfect.

Reflective Text
2 Corinthians 12:1-10

It is necessary to boast; nothing is to be gained by it, but I will go on to visions and revelations of the Lord. I know a person in Christ who fourteen years ago was caught up to the third heaven—whether in the body or out of the body I do not know; God knows. And I know that such a person—whether in the body or out of the body I do not know; God knows—was caught up into Paradise and heard things that are not to be told, that no mortal is permitted to repeat. On behalf of such a one I will boast, but on my own behalf I will not boast, except of my weaknesses. But if I wish to boast, I will not be a fool, for I will be speaking the truth. But I refrain from it, so that no one may think better of me than what is seen in me or heard from me, even considering the exceptional character of the revelations. Therefore, to keep me from being too elated, a thorn was given me in the flesh, a messenger of Satan to torment me, to keep me from being too elated. Three times I appealed to the Lord about this, that it would leave me, but he said to me, "My grace is sufficient for you, for power is made perfect in weakness." So, I will boast all the more gladly of my weaknesses, so that the power of Christ may dwell in me. Therefore I am content with weaknesses, insults, hardships, persecutions, and calamities for the sake of Christ; for whenever I am weak, then I am strong.

Prayer
Heavenly Father, you made Jesus weak. You made him as helpless as anyone lying on his or her death bed, except you put him on a cross so that we could watch.

Friends come by to see me and wish me well. I know they're glad it's not their time. They say dumb things. They cannot hear themselves. It doesn't matter. They came, they tried, and they cared. They just didn't know what to say. Thank you for sending them.

Lord, I'm not strong enough any longer to appeal to you from strength. I just don't have much left. I have nothing to offer you. There are no good works left in me. I am spent.

To tell you the truth, I have a lot of regrets. I'm filled with stuff I'm trying to forget, and with all sorts of "I wish I had." I am no poet who can wax serene. I am no philosopher who hopes to impress students, even in dying, that I am someone special. I know who I am. I am weak and getting weaker. I am leaving this world. I don't want to leave behind all those whom I love.

I am looking for your grace, Lord. I am asking you for it. I need it and I want it and I am ready to let you have your way with me. I am sorry that I am doing this in my ultimate weakness, when I have no other choice. But you are kind. You are kinder than I am. And you are my king. I ask you to forgive me my wrongs and to make me new, in your likeness, like I've sometimes imagined I could be.

Lord, my body is no longer of use to me or to you. If all I've been is a body, I say farewell with ease. Nothing matters if that is so. But Lord, you are my king and I am your subject. You are my Lord and I am your child. Neither life nor dying body will separate us from one another. In this hope, I consign myself to you. Wake me in your likeness soon. Amen

---

Reflective Questions

1. "My thoughts are not your thoughts, nor are your ways my ways," says God in Isaiah 55:8. Why is this a hopeful thought for us?

2. Letting go of guilt is accepting God's kindness, even when we don't deserve it. Why is letting go of guilt so difficult?

3. When is the last time you asked for kindness from God?

7

Doing the Dying

Death appears flippant at times. For those who are old and in pain, the long process can be tortuous. For those who are young with a lifetime ahead of them, death can be a quick, unwelcome visitor. The church gives mixed messages about this. Sometimes death is called an enemy, like Scripture names it (see 1 Corinthians 15:26). Sometimes death is called a friend or merciful, especially when there is no possible hope for recovery or for quality of life.

As I write these words, I am waiting, impatiently, for the death of my mother. For more than a year she has weakened to the point of exhaustion and pain. Only morphine provides some questionable relief and extension of life. She weighs seventy pounds. Dad, the love of her life, died a year ago. I cannot see any purpose whatsoever in her continued suffering. She will never sit up again, much less go outside. When she can speak, it's about dark cellars or love for us all—back and forth she goes between confused and clear thoughts. I do not accept the premise that this is good timing, according to God's clock. On the contrary, I think it is the enemy, death, playing with lives. Why God permits this, I do not know.

I write these words in the midst of her dying because I do not want to gloss over the horrible feelings I have about this. It is enough for me to question the sovereignty, if not the love of God. I am afraid that if I write this later, I will be glib about dying, for the pain will be diminished with time. We often rationalize the awfulness of having a beloved one die. But today I feel anger and helplessness. I suspect, when it is all over, I will feel a measure of guilt, too, for being in a hurry to have this awfulness over.

This week I've had the opportunity to be with a pastor who was dying. I have been visiting with him regularly, for he said he liked to hear me pray. As he neared death, I told him that I was out of words. I told him that he had gone farther down this path than I had, that he would have to advise me of what he was experiencing. There was perpetual pain on his forehead. Touching him anywhere caused him to grimace. His voice had been taken away. He could not respond. I knew that I was one of his last links to this world. I served as one of the pallbearers at his funeral, carrying his body either to the pit of death or to the gate of eternal life.

Dear friends, we do not know for sure what is going on with our lives or with our deaths. It is an enigma. We know what Scripture says, and if we want, we can quote it all day long, pretending a strong faith that we do not have. We will not know how well we will die until we are there, doing our dying.

My mother smiled this week, like she has every week during the past year. It is only the presence of family that makes this occur.

My pastor friend also wanted his family nearby during his dying. They were there in force—wife, three sons, two young grandchildren. Presence is all we could offer. We had no power to hasten or delay death.

I have seen people die deaths worse than crucifixion. This is a hard thing to say, but I think it is true. We want to think that Jesus died the worst death possible. Only because he was innocent of sin can we say that his death was worse than others. Two thieves, on the same day as his dying, experienced an equal demise in terms of pain and suffering.

For us, usually, it is cancer doing the deed, but it could be AIDS or a host of other ailments, even old age. The suffering is extended for months and months. How then can we approach the throne of God, with all these beloved ones ready for the chariot to eternal life, when no chariot seems available for boarding?

Job, of course, had this experience, as did Jonah. Job, because of his sufferings, cursed the day of his birth. Jonah was ready to be thrown into the sea for relief. Three times he wished to die. Both Job and Jonah were looking for an exit that was denied. Both had to wait for a better solution to their problem.

Reflective Text

Job 3:1-11

After this Job opened his mouth and cursed the day of his birth. Job said:

"Let the day perish in which I was born,
and the night that said,
'A man-child is conceived.' Let that day be darkness!
May God above not seek it,
or light shine on it.
Let gloom and deep darkness claim it.
Let clouds settle upon it;
let the blackness of the day terrify it.
That night—let thick darkness seize it!
let it not rejoice among the days of the year;
let it not come into the number of the months.
Yes, let that night be barren;
let no joyful cry be heard in it.
Let those curse it who curse the Sea,
those who are skilled to rouse up Leviathan.
Let the stars of its dawn be dark;
let it hope for light, but have none;
may it not see the eyelids of the morning—
because it did not shut the doors of my mother's womb,
and hide trouble from my eyes.
"Why did I not die at birth,
come forth from the womb and expire?"

Jonah 1:5-12

Then the mariners were afraid, and each cried to his god. They threw the cargo that was in the ship into the sea, to lighten it for them. Jonah, meanwhile, had gone down into the hold of the ship and had lain down, and was fast asleep. The captain came and said to him, "What are you doing sound asleep? Get up, call on your god! Perhaps the god will spare us a thought so that we do not perish."

The sailors said to one another, "Come, let us cast lots, so that we may know on whose account this calamity has come upon us." So they cast lots, and the lot fell on Jonah. Then they said to him, "Tell us why this calamity has come upon us. What is your occupation? Where do you come from? What is your country? And of what people are you?" "I am a Hebrew," he replied. "I worship the Lord, the God of heaven, who made the sea and the dry land." Then the men were even more afraid, and said to him, "What is this that you have done!" For the men knew that he was fleeing from the presence of the Lord, because he had told them so.

Then they said to him, "What shall we do to you, that the sea may quiet down for us?" For the sea was growing more and more tempestuous. He said to them, "Pick me up and throw me into the sea; then the sea will quiet down for you; for I know it is because of me that this great storm has come upon you."

Prayer

Merciful God, like Job and Jonah, I struggle with what is happening in my life. I don't know what you're doing to me or to those whom I love. I am ready for an exit. I see no purpose for the turmoil and distress that has come upon me or upon those whom I love. I wonder about you.

Lord, it is you to whom I am talking—no one else. It is you to whom my heart is directed—no one else. If you are not there and if I do not matter, so be it. I will lay down my life and let the sea wash over me. I will quit this life and relinquish all. I will say that I was a fool for the faith; I was mistaken.

Why, Lord, can't I let go of you? Why can't I jump from the ship, curse the day of my birth, and be done with you? Why can't I wash my hands and say with Pilate, "I am through with you." Why don't you exit from my life like I would exit from this world—quickly, easily, painlessly?

It is the other battle, isn't it? It's the grudge between yourself and the evil one. It's the wager you have. It's the balance beam. It's the contest of powers in worlds I know nothing about. It's you and Satan, pure and simple, at odds with one another, and we humans are the prize.

Some prize.

I am not worthy of the effort. Though made in your image, after your likeness, I do not sense that I am of that much value in the cosmic sense of things. You, with your eons, and I, with my few years, are hardly in the same camp.

It's about you, isn't it, Lord, and not about me? It's all about principalities and powers. I feel like a pawn on a chess board. Expendable. Except for the image thing you did. You made me in your image. You made me to be like you. You put faith into my heart that there is a kingdom, and I cannot deny it—though I might want to. It is such a little faith, such a little flame, such a little tree, such a little kingdom, but if it is yours I will go with it, simply because (and this is not flattery) I have no place else to go. To hell with Satan; that's what I say. Let Satan hold back death and the gate of heaven. You will not be denied.

But Lord, sooner rather than later is what I wish. Amen

Reflective Questions

1. The twin mysteries of life and death often make us ask foolish questions. How might we embrace God's mysteries as both mighty ways beyond our understanding and love-filled?

2. In what ways have you reconciled your anger toward God over the death of a loved one? If you are still angry, what would help you to move past the anger?

3. How does it feel to be a part of God's cosmic battle against the prince of darkness? Helpless? Important? What else?

8

When God Says "No"

All of us have prayed prayers that didn't work. We've asked for this or that, given solutions to God that were not needed, and sometimes even begged for things to go a certain way. But this or that didn't come, the problem wasn't solved, and the begging didn't bring God into the drama of our lives as we wanted. What are we to say about this? Does prayer only work some of the time? Doesn't God hear us when we pray wrongly? These types of thoughts need to be faced directly. Pretending that we have never been disappointed in our prayer life is probably not an honest admission for most of us.

Jesus invites us to pray in his name (John 14:14). We may not use that exact phrase, but there is an implied understanding that prayer is not a way to get our way, but a way to be in touch with Jesus. Prayer is not an attempt to get God on our side. God is already on our side. We are children of God. Rather, prayer makes a personal need a family matter. When we pray, we ask God to give us the power to see divine care in our pressing concern.

Praying in the name of Jesus is saying, "God, I really don't know what is best in this situation. I know how I feel and I know what I want, but I do not know what is best." These are hard words to pray when pain and loss are on the line. It's even harder to say, "Not my will, but yours be done" (Luke 22:42). But when we go to the head of the family, we go as children of the Heavenly Father, and not as the parent of God.

Sometimes we create prayer chains. If we do so believing that we can bombard the gates of heaven with so many pleas for help or healing that God cannot say no, then we have misunderstood prayer. God isn't deaf. One open heart to God is more powerful than ten thousand prayers without openness. God has the keenest ear possible. God can hear us praying when we aren't praying words! God senses our needs, our misery, and our inability to express our anguish, before words ever form in our mouths. God constantly listens to our hearts, whether we vocalize our thoughts or not. Christ even promised to send us the Holy Spirit to pray for us when we do not know what to say.

Why pray vocally then? Because God expects us to try to put into words what is in our hearts. When we say it clearly, then there is something on the table between us—a starting point for conversation. When we say our prayer aloud, we can finally hear for ourselves what is in our own mind and heart. God will help us hear it and help us to see what we're really saying.

Our spoken prayer is not to clarify God's mind and heart, but our own. Spoken prayer begins to clarify the confusion in our own minds and the fear in our own hearts. When we pray with words, God has access to us, and we can begin to hear our own heart, our own needs, and our own fears. When we ask God "What do you think?" God has a beginning place to make a response.

Admittedly, getting our own way, especially in matters of life and death for ourselves or for one we love, is very important. Not often would we be able to say to God, "Ok, it's time for me to die," or, "I see it's time for my loved one to go on." In old age or in deep suffering we might get to that point, but if God answered "yes" to every prayer for complete restoration to health and continued long life, then hardly anyone would ever die—or need the resurrection.

Getting our own way is not the object of prayer. Prayer is deliberately asking God to be involved in our lives and in the lives of those whom we love. It may include an ardent request for God to perform a miracle. God will take that under consideration. Our requests are respected. God listens closely to our petitions and loves intercessory prayer, because it's usually for someone other than us. But God reminds us to remember that we have seen only a small part of the kingdom. This world is only a fragment of what is yet to come.

Reflective Text

Matthew 7:7-12

[Jesus said,] "Ask, and it will be given you; search, and you will find; knock, and the door will be opened for you. For everyone who asks receives, and everyone who searches finds, and for everyone who knocks, the door will be opened. Is there anyone among you who, if your child asks for bread, will give a stone? Or if the child asks for a fish, will give a snake? If you then, who are evil, know how to give good gifts to your children, how much more will your Father in heaven give good things to those who ask him!

"In everything do to others as you would have them do to you; for this is the law and the prophets."

Prayer

Lord, your silence sounds like your "no." Kneeling before you in church or praying at home seems frustratingly futile. Sometimes it seems as though my prayers go nowhere. Sometimes it seems as though there is only emptiness and void, not a loving Father or a present Son or any kind of a comforting Spirit.

I think, perhaps, that I am praying wrongly. I wonder if there are better words, or if I need a more sincere heart. I wonder why some seem to have the gift of communication with you while I do not.

In your own words in Matthew's gospel, you tell me that everyone who asks will receive. You say that you will open the door to everyone who knocks. Everyone who searches finds, you say, yet sometimes, maybe many times, it doesn't seem as though this is true.

How, Lord, am I to set aside my feelings and instead, trust your presence? How am I to get beyond brain prayer and trust your promises? It is so hard for me to let go of the tools of normal conversation between people, and accept the fact that prayer is deeper than this, deeper than words and thoughts, holy.

Lord, I come asking for your good gifts—the best you have. Because I do not know much beyond the gifts of this world, please open my heart to sense gifts beyond understanding, ready for opening when you're ready to declare that the time is right. The storehouse of your wisdom, the depths of your mercy, the power of your healing, and your ultimate supremacy over death fills me with delight, and I look forward to the time when you say in clarity, "Child of mine, get up and come with me." Then shall the door be open and my questions will cease. Then I will see you face to face and grin from ear to ear. Then all the nonsense of this world will dissipate, like morning dew. In that coming day I trust. Today, I ask for strength sufficient for this day's challenges. Amen

---

Reflective Questions

1. What does it mean to pray in the name of Jesus? Why is it important?
2. If God knows all, why bother to pray?
3. How much comfort do you receive from knowing that the Holy Spirit prays for you and with you?

9

Prime Time

What the world understands as the prime time of our earth years only lasts a couple of decades at most. Pick the best twenty years for yourself. Everything else either leads up to or away from this time.

What is meaningful human life? Is prime time the highs of our lives or our lows? Like the person suffering from bipolar disorder, we like to think that we are at our norm when we are at our best. Maybe we are also at our norm at other points on the spectrum. The hard times may not be the most exhilarating times of our lives, but they are probably closer to the real norm of being human than our occasional highs.

The world's view of what it means to be living in prime time becomes most clear when we consider the destitute of the world, the people who never seem to enjoy life's high times. Who can really see, in the swollen belly of a hungry child, a human as prized as the Christ-child in the manger? Who can see in the face of an African child, deceased because of AIDS, a real child of God being borne to a resurrection tomb? We may not see them as Christ's lights because they appear too pathetic to be human. We value those who accomplish great things.

As Christians, we know that prime time is any time in God's time. In prime time, God recognizes us for who we are and not for what we do. God says, "You are mine." The greatest in the history of humankind have not been persons like Alexander the Great, Napoleon, or the great thinkers of the ages. Rather, as Christians we remember Mother Teresa. We think of Job when he's destitute. We think of King David without Absalom, Abraham contemplating life without Isaac, Mary at the foot of the cross losing her son, Jesus welcoming the outcasts. These are our models.

There are probably not a lot of conversions in what the world sees as life's prime time. Why should there be? We are pretty self-sufficient then. We rarely need any outside help. The very young and the very old have no such self-sufficiency. When we are in those stages of life, God intervenes and says, "Your crib is my manger; your tomb is my tomb." Dear pilgrim, we have a God with whom it's worth spending the night, the week, our life on earth, and our eternal life, in honest loving companionship.

Reflective Text
Ecclesiastes 3:1-11

For everything there is a season, and a time for every matter under heaven:
a time to be born, and a time to die;
a time to plant, and a time to pluck up what is planted;
a time to kill, and a time to heal;
a time to break down, and a time to build up;
a time to weep, and a time to laugh;
a time to mourn, and a time to dance;
a time to throw away stones,
    and a time to gather stones together;
a time to embrace, and a time to refrain from embracing;
a time to seek, and a time to lose;
a time to keep, and a time to throw away;
a time to tear, and a time to sew;
a time to keep silence, and a time to speak;
a time to love, and a time to hate;
a time for war, and a time for peace.

What gain have the workers from their toil? I have seen the business that God has given to everyone to be busy with. He has made everything suitable for its time; moreover he has put a sense of past and future into their minds, yet they cannot find out what God has done from the beginning to the end.

Prayer

Lord, I know that I have to die before you can make me rise to new life. I don't like this fact. I've tried dying little deaths to myself through the years, but the big one, the last one, the real one is terrifying for some of us.

Lord, I also know that life on earth and in the universe occurred eons before I was awakened to the reality of it all. Sometimes I think you may have made a mistake by waking me—or any of us—up to this physical world of brawn and beauty, of sin and grace, of hate and love.

Yet, here I am, having had the experience of the manger by becoming human, but not yet able to imagine my empty tomb. That tomb or ground or sea that swallows up what little is left of my body after death is no comforter. The ground is cold, the sea forever swirls, and the wind forever scatters. How shall I be made again? How will you gather my remains and with a word resurrect me? When will the warmth return to me, with strength and life and joy and family?

All these things you have already done for me once, in my birth. In this I take my comfort. Before I had a notion of life, you formed me from the dust of the earth and in my mother's womb. It was all gift, all grace. You gave me breath and opened my eyes, and then my heart. You dared even to use me in your work on earth. You made many promises to me, and you have kept them all. It's the promise of resurrection that I struggle to believe. I ask for your help in my unbelief.

My manger was really your manger, Lord. You are there. My tomb is really your tomb, Lord, and you are there. Death always flees from your presence, just as it had to flee from your Son in the borrowed tomb in the Easter cemetery.

Lord, you need nothing to resurrect me. The only need is who you are: Love Incarnate, Power Infinite, Faithfulness Profound. Receive me into your eternal care. Amen

---

Reflective Questions

1. Is it an insult to God to confess the same sin repeatedly, as though God has not yet forgiven it? Why or why not?
2. Why is it often harder for us to believe that God loves us individually as much as God loves the world?
3. What have been the "prime times" in your life with God?

10

The Christian Funeral

The Christian funeral is unlike any other funeral. We grieve deeply, but not as those who have no hope. We believe it is good to grieve, because Christ promises a happiness and a blessedness to those who grieve, not to those who refuse to grieve. It is also coming to terms with the fact that we are living in enemy-occupied territory, where our three enemies (sin, death, and the devil) still prevail.

Grieving is a necessary experience. Even Jesus did it on more than one occasion. In Luke 19:41-42, right before he cast the money changers out of the temple, he grieved over Jerusalem: "As he came near and saw the city, he wept over it, saying, 'If you, even you, had only recognized on this day the things that make for peace! But now they are hidden from your eyes.'"

Jesus also wept over the death of his friend Lazarus. Twice in the long drama of the story of the raising of Lazarus from the dead, we read these amazing responses of Jesus: "Jesus began to weep," (John 11:35) and "Then Jesus, again greatly disturbed, came to the tomb. It was a cave, and a stone was lying against it" (John 11:38).

Jesus's grief is real grief, even though he had the power to restore Lazarus to earthly life. Some scholars speculate that Jesus grieved because he was going to bring Lazarus back from a better place, to this place, with the necessity that Lazarus would have to die again someday, since this would not be the resurrection to eternal life. Others simply see it as great love and affection for a friend, along with pure empathy with many others who were grieving, especially Mary and Martha, the sisters of Lazarus.

Grieving is coming to terms with what an awesome gift we had been given and, for a time, must relinquish. In our grieving we may regret that we didn't value the loved one more than we did, but that is not really helpful grieving . . . that is simply "guilting." No one ever loved another person perfectly. We don't need grief to teach us this. Rather, grieving is recognizing the beauty of the deceased. It's as though we discover that the loved one was no mere animal-being, but a presentation of the love of Christ in human form into our own lives. Love was shared. Since God is love, the source of the love is God. Therefore, we are not merely yielding up ashes to ashes and dust to dust in our grieving. We are committing the whole person— body, mind, and spirit—into the loving care of God.

The commendation sentence used at many Christian funerals says this very well: "Into your hands, O merciful Savior, we commend your servant, (baptismal name). Acknowledge, we humbly beseech you, a sheep of your own fold, a lamb of your own flock, a sinner of your own redeeming. Receive him/her into the arms of your mercy, into the blessed rest of everlasting peace, and into the glorious company of the saints in light" (*Lutheran Book of Worship*, page 211).

That said, there are other elements of the funeral service that have been largely neglected in the more traditional Christian denominations, and too much emphasized in other Christian denominations. It's as if one group of denominations was trying to swing the pendulum too far to the other side for the sake of compensating for the excesses of the other.

There is no need to ignore the deceased at the time of the funeral celebration meditation. He/she has a name, and it needs to be spoken aloud, maybe more than once or twice. Yet many traditional churches, believing heartily and rightly that the resurrection of Christ must be proclaimed above all else, can conduct a funeral in such a way as to make the deceased person anonymous, and their contribution to God's purpose, or God's work through them, inscrutable, nonexistent, of no moment. Conversely, other denominations can use the occasion of the funeral as an attempt to scare persons into the faith (lest such a moment as this overcome the listener unawares) or, even worse, preach the deceased person into heaven. All three of these approaches miss the mark. To make the person anonymous, a hero/heroine, or an example of "what not to be" is not the point of a Christian celebration. Each, in its own sinister way, is avoiding the reality of the death of the deceased, the work God has done through this person, and joyful thanksgiving for his or her life.

The Christian funeral meditation is a time to recognize that God has used this person, that there is good grieving occurring (which means that there is worth), and that God's grace was at work in this life, possibly through many decades of living, and possibly during a much shorter period of time.

Preparing for one's own Christian funeral is not as morbid a thought as one might at first suspect. As one who has done it, I can testify to its value. I know what I hope the ceremony might be—joyful, filled with thanksgiving, with some quiet time during a powerful vibrant organ solo, for reflection upon the new life each of us can expect as resurrected children of the Heavenly Father. There are selections of Scripture, hymns, and special music. The meditation itself, of course, must be left to another to compose. However, the aforementioned items should be a very helpful guide for the pastor in preparing a message.

The tone of the funeral is that of a celebratory worship service that takes a look at the new life to come. This means that death does not have the last word—Christ does. His word will be, "Get up." His word will be a resurrection word to eternal life, not a restoration to earthly life. The funeral is a time to celebrate, grieve, and to give thanks for what has been. It is also a time to look forward to the great reunion, when Christ keeps his promises to bring us to the place of many mansions, but more importantly, to the Great Reunion, complete with banquet and song.

It is important for the pastor conducting the funeral to have had some lengthy conversation with the surviving members of the family. Indeed, they will virtually write the funeral meditation for the pastor, if the pastor will unabashedly make notes, and incorporate the feelings and insights into the resurrection sermon.

Following is an example of a Christian funeral celebration meditation for a young man named Edward, who was killed in an automobile accident. It is printed here as a way to illustrate the involvement of the deceased with the still worshiping congregation on this side of the resurrection. Edward's father wrote one of the endorsements on the back cover of this book.

Funeral Sermon for Edward

The questions for this difficult day are mostly in these three texts: The first is from Isaiah 40:28-31.

Have you not known? Have you not heard? The Lord is the everlasting God, the Creator of the ends of the earth. He does not faint or grow weary; his understanding is unsearchable. He gives power to the faint, and strengthens the powerless. Even youths will faint and be weary, and the young will fall exhausted; but those who wait for the Lord shall renew their strength, they shall mount up with wings like eagles, they shall run and not be weary, they shall walk and not faint.

The second set of questions are from Romans 8:31-39.

What then are we to say about these things? If God is for us, who is against us? He who did not withhold his own Son, but gave him up for all of us, will he not with him also give us everything else? Who will bring any charge against God's elect? It is God who justifies. Who is to condemn? It is Christ Jesus, who died, yes, who was raised, who is at the right hand of God, who indeed intercedes for us. Who will separate us from the love of Christ? Will hardship, or distress, or persecution, or famine, or nakedness, or peril, or sword? As it is written, "For your sake we are being killed all day long; we are accounted as sheep to be slaughtered." No, in all these things we are more than conquerors through him who loved us. For I am convinced that neither death, nor life, nor angels, nor rulers, nor things present, nor things to come, nor powers, nor height, nor depth, nor anything else in all creation, will be able to separate us from the love of God in Christ Jesus our Lord.

The third text for the sermon is from John 14:1-6.

Jesus counsels us, "Do not let your hearts be troubled. Believe in God, believe also in me. In my Father's house there are many dwelling places. If it were not so, would I have told you that I go to prepare a place for you? And if I go and prepare a place for you, I will come again and will take you to myself, so that where I am, there you may be also. And you know the way to the place where I am going." Thomas said to him, "Lord, we do not know where you are going. How can we know the way?" Jesus said to him, "I am the way, and the truth, and the life. No one comes to the Father except through me."

We heard two questions from Isaiah: "Have you not known? Have you not heard? The Lord is the everlasting God, the Creator of the ends of the earth."

We also heard two questions from Psalm 139: "Where can I go then from your Spirit? Where can I flee from your presence? If I climb up to heaven, you are there; if I make the grave my bed, you are there also."

Three questions came to us from Paul: "What then are we to say about these things? If God is for us, who is against us? He who did not withhold his own Son, but gave him up for all of us, will he not with him also give us everything else?"

Seven questions! And not all of Paul's questions were even read! We could add seven thousand more questions to those posed by Isaiah, the Psalmist, and by Paul, because we are deeply grieved today.

Edward, Edward, we are going to miss you, but not as those who have no hope.

When we grieve for you, dear Edward, your Lord and our Lord promises that we will be blessed: "Blessed are those who grieve, for they will be comforted."

"What can we say?" Paul asks us, in this life and death passage from Romans 8. "Who can be against us if God is for us?" Will he not with him give us everything else? Everyone else back?

The one question, unanswerable in many respects, but still in our hearts and minds is "Why?" "Why, Lord, this day, this beautiful life cut short?"

We, of course, do not believe that God needed another "little angel" in heaven.

We do not believe that Edward's time had come. We do not believe that this, in any way, is the will of God.

So, we are rather stymied with the "Why" question from a spiritual point of view.

For the answer to this question we have to look to science, of all things . . . the way the world works, the way earth and its beings are put together.

"Why?" is a physical question, not a spiritual one. When an accident happens, laws of physics apply. "Why, 'death,' in an accident?"

Because we have a body.

It's the same thing when deadly diseases develop and the young die too soon. The laws of medicine then apply, because we have a body.

When tragedy strikes, and the innocent die, it's because we have a body. This is the plain, hard-and-fast rule of living as a human.

So, let us put the question of "why" on the shelf and leave it there, because, quite frankly, it is a lousy question on a day like this one, and it seeks to block us from spiritual considerations. It's Satan's question, who wants us to doubt the love of God. It's him saying, "How could your God do such an awful thing to the one you love?"

Be gone, Satan. Out of here. This is the Body of Christ—his church—his people. Be gone! Unless you've come to worship Almighty God, whose eyes see even the death of the elderly as tragic, and has done something about it.

Now, then, let us talk to God the Father about this matter, and to Jesus Christ who tells us, "Do not let your hearts be troubled."

Instead of "why?" let us ask the other more important questions, the spiritual ones that Isaiah, the Psalmist, and Paul address, and Jesus, himself, experiences . . . the questions we want to ask.

I. "What?" is the first question.

It's Paul's question given to us: "What, then, can we say about this thing called death?"

I suppose, if we're really honest, we would frame the question in an even more difficult way: "What are we going to do, Lord, with this horrible burden?" "What are you going to do, Lord, to help us with this horrible burden?"

Some of you know what primitive homemade tools are. A human yoke is one of them. It fits well. I remember seeing a woman use a yoke to haul water up from the creek in front of her house, because she didn't have running water. She was elderly and frail. As late as the mid 1960s you could see this woman carrying water up from the creek, a bucket on each end of the yoke.

It was still plenty heavy, she explained, but the balance was better than trying to carry the water by hand. The weight was on her shoulders—and besides, you didn't have to fill those buckets up to the brim!

We, mature people of the faith, and youngsters just starting out, sometimes think we can bear burdens all by ourselves. Just give me a good-fitting yoke.

How foolish of us.

How proud.

How we wish to make it without the Lord's help. But the Lord says, "No. Not this burden. It doesn't fit in buckets, and it's far to heavy for a human yoke."

"What are you going to do, Lord, to help us with this horrible burden?"

When Jesus told us to take his yoke upon us, "because his burden is easy and his yoke is light," he was saying, "Dear people of God. I know you can't plow the earthly field alone. I know it's too much for you to bear alone. I know your limitations. I don't expect you to be Hercules. I don't want you to be Atlas. I just ask you to let me be yoked with you. Let me under your yoke . . . let your yoke be my yoke. See me along side of you. It's a double yoke, don't you see? Not a single. Let me do the pulling and the lifting, step by step, with you. I am taller than you. I can lift more of the load. I promise you, that my Father and I weep with you. I promise you, that the Holy Spirit hears your moans and groans and your sighs too deep for words. I promise you that Father, Son, and Holy Spirit love you and your loved one, now and forever."

That's "what" we will say about these things. Slide the yoke over. For God's sake, and your own, make some yoke room.

II. We move on to a second question, "Where?"

Again we turn to Paul to begin our answer who is writing to the Corinthians. Today all of us are honorary Corinthians. Hear what Paul writes to us about "where?": "Where, O death, is your victory? Where, O death, is your sting?" The sting of death is sin, and the power of sin is the law. But thanks be to God, who gives us the victory through our Lord Jesus Christ" (1 Cor 15:55-57).

Again, we might ask the question even more personally: "Where" are those who were given to us in love but have been lost in death?"

Because you and I are still in our bodies, we think of "place" as "physical place." It's all we know. It's the question we answer on cell phones when someone calls in—"where" are you.

And the question is answered, "I'm at . . . wherever the place is . . . on the road, at somebody's house, in a store, wherever."

But the Psalmist asks the question better and nudges us away from "place" to "person."

"Where can I go then from your Spirit? Where can I flee from your presence? If I climb up to heaven, you are there; if I make the grave my bed, you are there also" (Psalm 139:7-8).

Our problem isn't trying to find God somewhere, it's getting rid of God, pretending God isn't in that yoke with us.

It can't be done.

We can't get away from God, even when we want to. The Psalmist says it in again and again: "you are there."

"Yea though I walk through the valley of the shadow of death, you are there."

And Jesus says it too: "Lo, I am with you always, to the close of the age."

I'll be there.

And Jesus also says, to make sure there is a place, and we can understand it, "Lo, I go to prepare a place for you, that where I am you may be also . . . for eternity."

Place is the person of Jesus Christ. Jesus Christ is the answer to the question of "where?"

III. What and Where, now "How?"

How does all of this happen?

We're not the first persons to ask this question, and again, we have to move away from the physical to the Spiritual. Psalm 139 helps us see "how" God was working on us, and for us, before we were even born. The psalmist talks directly to God about it: "For it was you [God] who formed my inward parts; you knit me together in my mother's womb. I praise you, for I am fearfully and wonderfully made. Wonderful are your works; that I know very well. My frame was not hidden from you, when I was being made in secret, intricately woven in the depths of the earth. Your eyes beheld my unformed substance. In your book were written all the days that were formed for me, when none of them as yet existed. How weighty to me are your thoughts, O God! How vast is the sum of them! I try to count them—they are more than the sand; I come to the end—I am still with you."

Poor souls who think that life in the womb is a mere physical event. Poor souls who think that death ends everything, much less anything.

You just heard the psalmist's words. Hear them again: "I come to the end—I am still with you."

The "unformed substance" is back in the hands of God, that Great Potter and Creator of all.

And St. Paul, again writing to us in 1 Corinthians says, "But someone will ask, 'How are the dead raised? With what kind of body do they come?' Fool! What you sow does not come to life unless it dies. . . . Not all flesh is alike. . . . There are both heavenly bodies and earthly bodies . . . So it is with the resurrection of the dead. What is sown is perishable, what is raised is imperishable. . . . It is sown a physical body, it is raised a spiritual body. If there is a physical body, there is also a spiritual body . . ." (1 Corinthians 15:35-36, 40, 42, 44).

"How" we want to know. It's the question of Nicodemus in John 3: "How can anyone be born after having grown old?"

And Jesus says: "What is born of the flesh is flesh, and what is born of the Spirit is spirit."

And Nicodemus said to him, "How can these things be?"

And Jesus in frustration turns the "how" question back on Nicodemus: "If I have told you about earthly things and you do not believe, how can you believe if I tell you about heavenly things?"

And Jesus doesn't stop there. He goes on to some of the most momentous passages of Scripture in the whole Bible. To Nicodemus he continues: "How, you ask? This isn't going to be pretty, Nicodemus, but just as Moses lifted up the serpent in the wilderness, so must I be lifted up, that whoever believes in me may have eternal life."

How does this belief bring eternal life, you ask? By love. By the Heavenly Father's pure love.

Jesus continues: "For God so loved the world that he gave his only Son, so that everyone who believes in him may not perish but may have eternal life" (John 3:16).

Nicodemus, are you listening? It's a "heavenly matter"—and our loved one is "heavenly matter" now.

IV. Fourth question. "When?"

When we will see our loved ones again?

Waiting is not easy for us, especially when we have sought for and have had so many instant gratifications in our lives. But the great reunion is coming—"soon, and very soon." Still, we have to remember the words of Jesus: "But about that day and hour no one knows, neither the angels of heaven, nor the Son, but only the Father" (Matthew 24:36).

Paul, again writing to all of us Corinthians does give us this good news about "when." "Listen, I will tell you a mystery! We will all be changed, in a moment, in the twinkling of an eye, at the last trumpet. For the trumpet will sound, and the dead will be raised imperishable, and we will be changed" (1 Cor. 15:51-52).

V. Who

The last of our questions today is the most important of them all, and the most difficult to accept and accomplish, but you will.

Who?

Who is going to take care of Edward now? Who is going to love him like we did, like you did?

The short answer is the same God who created him, who loved him, along with us, who was always by his side, under his yoke, during his childhood health problems, during his play (what a grand smile!), in his work and in his worry, in his joys and in his sorrows, in his listening ear for his friends, in his humor, and in his caring heart for all of us.

But the "who" question goes much further than this. It's not just "who" is going to love Edward now? We can still do that too. We will do it.

Loving Edward is not God's prerogative alone. God wants us and expects us to love Edward always, and we will. The question is, the big question for all of us is, "Who are we after all?"

Or, better yet, "Whose are we?"

Father Abraham had to ask that hard question about his only son, Isaac: "God, you want me to offer him up forever? Whose son is this whom I love so dearly?"

Mother Mary had to ask it about Jesus: "Whose son is this whom I birthed? Do I have to offer him up forever?"

In both cases, the answer is "No, you don't."

We have to ask it about our own beloved children. Whose child is this really . . . who had the power to give a gift so precious as this?

We even have to ask it about our parents: Who gave us these older persons of our lives, our mothers, our fathers, our guardians?

We have to ask it about our brothers and sisters: Whose sister is this? Whose brother?

We have to ask it about our best friends, Whose friend is this?

We even have to ask it about our beloved spouses: Whose wife, whose husband is this?

To whom do all these people really belong? We finally even have to ask it about ourselves. Whose am I, Lord?

Scripture tells us very plainly that we are not our own. Scripture tells us that our very bodies are temples. Scripture tells us that God the Father and Jesus the Christ through the power of the Holy Spirit claims each of us as their beloved child forever.

I know what is necessary for us to pray.

May God give us the courage and grace to pray it, one by one, regarding the horrible loss we mourn. Today may not be the day you'll be able to pray it, but I know that the day will come.

Your grief will be mighty, and you will pray to almighty God with Edward and agape love on your mind:

"God, take care of your son.

God, take care of your brother.

God, take care of your nephew, your cousin.

God, take care of your friend."

And when that day comes for us, one by one, when we realize that we can no longer care for Edward like we have in the past, when we realize that we love him more than ever, then, out of deep love for him, we will truly give Edward over to the loving care of God.

In that twinkling of an eye, our yoke will grow lighter, and we will get Edward back in a new light. We will be able to see Edward as alive again, not as someone we need to care for, but as our beloved equal, who loves us from the other side of death, as he lives in the presence of Almighty God, sitting at the table enjoying the fullness of the feast to come, waiting patiently for the rest of us to join with him at Christ's table in that great, great, great reunion day meal.

A closing note: Our final hymn this morning is "I Know That My Redeemer Lives." Powerful words, powerful hymn. It helps to recall where the words are from and who wrote them.

Those of us familiar with Scripture know about the long, long suffering of Job. The Book of Job is 42 chapters in length. Chapter 1 is a chapter of peace and serenity. Chapter 42 is a restoration of joy. Every other chapter in the book is one of burdensome pain and loss.

You might think that the words, "I know that my Redeemer lives" comes at the end of the book. It's not so. It comes right in the middle of the book . . . right in the middle of the suffering, and it doesn't end Job's suffering.

Listen to the words of Job, chapter 19 of the Book of Job, the most momentous statement of faith and joy in all of the Old Testament: "O that my words were written down! [They are!] O that they were inscribed in a book! [They are!] O that with an iron pen and with lead they were engraved on a rock forever! [They are in the Bible forever!] For I know that my Redeemer lives, and that at the last he will stand upon the earth; and after my skin has been thus destroyed, then in my flesh I shall see God, whom I shall see on my side, and my eyes shall behold, and not another. My heart faints within me!" (Job 19:23-27).

Let us prepare ourselves, in the midst of our grief, to remember the Amazing Grace Meal, the foretaste of the Feast to come, and then to sing, "I Know That My Redeemer Lives."

11

Coping with Grief

Coping almost always involves living with less than what we had before. The loss of a loved one, expected or unexpected, diminishes our family support network, regardless of the age of the deceased. How we go about changing our lives to adjust to the new reality is called coping, and it requires a lot of courage.

The various stages of grief have been well presented and are well worth knowing in advance of the time we become immersed in the grief process. However, a person in grief for the first time is not likely to be looking for explanations of their pain or their feelings. More likely, the person just wants the pain to stop, for the loved one to come back, for the death to be undone.

Those who do know the various stages of grief may wish to bypass a step or two and go straight to complete healing, which is not possible. Those who avoid their grief simply delay or postpone the healing process.

Often the very phrases *healing process* or *grief process* can be a turnoff. We resent having our pain called a process. We protest, "It's a person I lost, not a process to manage." When we hear that there are stages to our suffering, we might feel insulted. It makes everything appear clinical and not real.

Most persons who write about the stages of grief recognize that stages overlap, and they write compassionately. They explain that progress toward recovery can be much longer than the proverbial year of mourning.

Yet, we may have in our minds that we are different from others. We want to get on with our lives. We insist we have done enough suffering, but the loss keeps poking up its head as if to say, "Don't forget about me." For example, we might want to bypass the anger stage of grief by trying to be brave, philosophical, or deeply spiritual. Then, all of a sudden, we are angry. We are angry at God, angry at death, angry at the one who died for dying on us, angry at ourselves for not being stronger, angry at some other human being that irks us for no apparent reason. The list is endless.

Perhaps one of the worst phrases to hear when we are mourning is "Time heals all wounds." It's as though the idea is, "It's just a matter of the clock ticking off enough months and then you will forget your loss." It's not helpful, and it's not true. Time does pass, and grief does fade. But grief does not become more bearable just because time passes. The grief becomes more bearable because we change.

One of the things we can do that can help us cope with the pain we are feeling is to resist the notion that we need to forget about our loved one. It is advice that deserves our resentment. It is not possible to forget, it is not necessary to forget, and it is not right to forget. Our coping changes as we learn how to replace forgetting about our loved one with remembering the person in a new way. To forget our loved one is doing the wrong thing. To remember rightly brings healing.

Remembering rightly is to honestly wrestle with the future of our beloved. We might, for example, imagine what it would be like if our roles had been reversed. What if, for example, our beloved had to be doing what we're doing now, that is, mourning the loss of us? What if they were the survivor and we were not? How would they manage it, and how would we want them to manage it? Remembering them rightly may help us relieve an unnecessary burden we've placed on our own shoulders.

One of the great discoveries in grieving for our lost one is realizing that we are not just grieving over them, but more profoundly, our grieving is a gift of love to them! It is a beautiful gift. We love them still, as our tears indicate. They don't have to go through what we're going through. Thank God it's us and not them.

From this beautiful discovery, we can honestly take some steps away from constant sorrow by saying, "My loved one would not want me to be so forlorn." In a sense, we receive permission from them not to grieve as those who have no hope. We receive permission from them to look forward to being back in each other's presence in a new way. And we give them permission to enjoy the new life that God has given them. These are big steps that only love can take.

We can also make the offering, the ultimate offering. Giving up the one whom we loved so dearly into the hands of the Almighty is the biggest gift we will ever make. It's saying to God, "You care for my loved one, not because I don't love them anymore but because I do love both them and you immensely, and I understand that you can give the care that is needed better than I at this time." This is loving your beloved and loving God. It is trusting both of them. It is freeing both of them to be alive for the other.

In a way, this is part of what Abraham struggled with when he considered sacrificing his son, Isaac, on the altar. Abraham surely worried that he loved his son more than he loved God. His tortured mind made him think that he must trust God with Isaac's life. You will remember, however, how God interrupted Abraham, and stopped the sacrifice by providing a substitute offering for Isaac's life, namely a ram caught in a thorny thicket. Abraham got his son back, along with the gospel news that God doesn't work this way. God doesn't want us to sacrifice our beloved ones on earth. God wants us to trust him with our most precious ones in the hereafter, where the offering is appropriate.

Mary, the mother of Jesus, also had the terrifying experience of losing her son on the cruel Friday we now call Good Friday. Mary's experience, unlike Abraham's, went even further, for Jesus became the ram caught in the thicket. Jesus became the sacrifice for all who lose a loved one. Mary learned that her son was really God's Son. As God's Son, Jesus was also our son, for we are all children of the heavenly Father. Jesus sensed this clearly from the cross when he provided for Mary's future with John, the beloved disciple: "Woman, here is your son [John]; Here is your mother [Mary]" (John 19:26-27). Never again could Mary lose Jesus forever, for by Easter Sunday morning, three days later, on the day of resurrection, Mary got her son back, though her earthly sojourn was forever changed. How long Mary grieved his death is not known, of course, but remembering Jesus rightly had to be part of her new life.

As was said above, the giving up the one whom we loved so dearly into the hands of almighty God is the biggest gift we might ever make. We do not sacrifice them on an altar out of a mistaken sense of devotion, and we do not see them crucified for others, but we do release them into God's care. In so doing, we change the way we love them. It takes more love than ever.

Grieving is our evidence that we have been given a pearl of great price, a magnificent gem, a life of remarkable meaning to us. This grieving, this liquid evidence in tears, becomes a source of thanksgiving, proof that we really did love our beloved one. And more than this, our grief becomes proof that God gifted us with a beloved one. Is it not better to ask, "How could God have loved me so much as to have given me this person to love in my life on earth?" than to say, "Why did my loved one die?" What God has done for us, through the gift of our beloved, formed from the mere soil of the earth, is nothing compared to what God will do when we meet again in our resurrected bodies.

Coping with loss is coping with loneliness. One of the most poignant cartoons I ever saw was of an elderly lady standing in front of her television set in the evening, patting it on its top, and saying, "Night, night." We need other people. We need to be around others, even when our senses say, "Disappear into yourself."

Other people need us too, both our presence and our witness, be it ever so small. We note how others cope, and we learn from them. When we are grieving, we are one of the "others," and people are watching us. This does not mean we have to pretend anything. We know it's best to find a friend we trust and share our emotions. The most natural thing in all the world is to wait with others for big events. When we wait at the hospital with the excitement of a delivery time nearing or when we participate in the drama of watching children grow up, we know that these moments are best done with the support of others. So, too, our grieving should be shared with trusted others.

Coping also requires an active life. We find ways to contribute our gifts, talents, and time. We are freer than ever to do this once we get past the need for recognition. We don't wait to be asked, for the asking may never come. We just do it out of love and take pleasure in being useful. We don't do it for a thank you, for that may never come either. We do it out of thanksgiving to God.

Finally, coping requires a sense of expectation. We expect God to keep all the resurrection promises. We expect a great reunion. We expect to be resurrected ourselves, for that is the promise of God that has nothing to do with our worthiness. It is just grace. We expect God to take care of our loved ones and us, because God is graceful. We expect to be together again, not because we miss each other so much, but because God said that is what's coming.

If our loved one was no more that an animal, then our grieving would be vain, as would life itself. But the conviction comes that our loved one was a gift from God, which we did not deserve. So, too, grace will be there for us, as surely as God is good.

Reflective Text
1 Thessalonians 4:13-18

But we do not want you to be uninformed, brothers and sisters, about those who have died, so that you may not grieve as others do who have no hope. For since we believe that Jesus died and rose again, even so, through Jesus, God will bring with him those who have died. For this we declare to you by the word of the Lord, that we who are alive, who are left until the coming of the Lord, will by no means precede those who have died. For the Lord himself, with a cry of command, with the archangel's call and with the sound of God's trumpet, will descend from heaven, and the dead in Christ will rise first. Then we who are alive, who are left, will be caught up in the clouds together with them to meet the Lord in the air; and so we will be with the Lord forever. Therefore encourage one another with these words.

Prayer

Lord Jesus Christ, I hurt so badly. Everything is lost. It's hard to find joy for even a moment. When it comes, it darts away again, like something sly, not to be trusted. If I laugh, I fear you will take away even this brief moment of happiness. If I smile, I wonder if it's denial. Everything seems so furtive, temporary, and unreal.

Sometimes I blame you for it all. You could have spent one more miracle. Sometimes I blame myself, wondering what I should have done differently. How many times I have said, "If only."

Lord, how will I ever cope with the "might have beens?" I will never stop thinking about the world we dreamed of together, with so many precious events forever ended. It is too much to bear, and I don't want to go on. I just want to wake up, turn the clock back, and have a second chance at life.

I don't like the word *cope*. It sounds like crawling, instead of walking. It makes me feel like I'm mentally ill and spiritually sick. I want to be brave and strong, a model of endurance, stoic to the end, but I can't do it. It isn't me. It isn't real.

Lord, this is not self pity. It is pity for the one who's gone, for what they're missing, for what they will never have on this earth.

There. I said it. I wanted life for them, as well as life with them. If that's not love, what is?

It is too hard to sing with tears on my cheek and lumps in my throat. But I will listen to the voices of those nearby. I will let them sing for me. I will let them pray for me. I am out of words, out of hope, out of strength to mourn more.

Lord, I need you. I need you to love the one that you gave me as much as I loved them. I need you to tell me that we've not seen the last of each other. I need you to give me a faith I don't feel I have right now. I need you to tell me that you love me too. Amen

---

Reflective Questions

1. What words and actions have been helpful to you in grieving?
2. What do you really want to say to God about your loss? What do you suppose the God of love might say in response to you?
3. Who do you want to sit next to at the great reunion table?

12

In Time

Elaine is an elderly woman, my senior by a generation. She is the kind of person who has a perpetual smile. Often that kind of person can grate on you, if you're not able to wear such a smile yourself, but Elaine is much too genuine not to be admired. There is no doubt about her life experience, her touch with reality. Elaine shows up for celebrations of all kinds—Sunday worship, weddings, even funeral celebrations that rejoice in the coming resurrection.

Not long ago, Elaine attended a wedding for dear friends, where I happened to be involved in a leadership capacity. The small clapboard country church is nestled in the mountains of southwest Virginia. To get into the church one has to climb about fifteen wooden steps; it's not very accessible to people who are physically challenged.

After the wedding we were out in front sending the newlyweds off to a new life together, and the people began to disperse. I noticed Elaine eyeing the hill she was about to climb to get to her car with her friend. Trying to be helpful, I asked, "Elaine, how far up there is your car?"

"Toward the top," she responded, arm in arm with her aged friend.

Thinking I might bring the car down to her I asked, "Can you make it?"

With confidence she responded, "In time."

The phrase has been a favorite of mine ever since, and I note its appropriateness to all sorts of situations.

A retired pastor called to tell me he was having difficulty preaching on the texts where ten maidens are waiting for the bridegroom to come. Five maidens were wise and five were foolish. He was clear about not wanting to use the text as a hammer to make people feel bad about not being prepared for the bridegroom who comes late. He was clear that he didn't want to preach guilt. He wanted to preach about the bridegroom who comes when his time is right.

I told him about Elaine and he understood. The bridegroom, Christ, does come, in time to his church and his people. That's the gospel.

From the time we first learned to hear the beat in music, we sensed that all of life has a rhythm. Sometimes the music director made us speed up or slow down in order to keep in time. If we stub our toe badly enough, it will throb, and we'll be reminded that our very body has a beat to it, too.

Scripture uses the phrase *in time* in interesting ways. It points to a future time, saying "the time to come" (Isaiah 30:8). But there is also reference to time past, with an admonition to remember God's faithfulness (for example, Psalm 106:43).

The phrase *in time of trouble* also occurs. Don't you just love to hear the vivid portrayal of a faithless friend being compared to a bad tooth? "Like a bad tooth or a lame foot is trust in a faithless person in time of trouble" (Proverbs 25:19).

When Jeremiah prayed about a drought he said, "Although our iniquities testify against us, act, O Lord . . . O hope of Israel, its savior in time of trouble, why should you be like . . . someone confused, like a mighty warrior who cannot give help? Yet you, O Lord, are in the midst of us, and we are called by your name; do not forsake us!" (Jeremiah 14:7-9). Despite the guilt of Jeremiah's people, Jeremiah pleads to God to do one thing: act. In time, God does.

In the New Testament, the author of Hebrews reminds us what kind of priest Christ is. The text says, "Since, then, we have a great high priest who has passed through the heavens, Jesus, the Son of God, let us hold fast to our confession. For we do not have a high priest who is unable to sympathize with our weaknesses, but we have one who in every respect has been tested as we are, yet without sin. Let us therefore approach the throne of grace with boldness, so that we may receive mercy and find grace to help in time of need" (Hebrews 4:14-16).

It goes without saying that we have many times of need—times of trouble, memories of good times past, and the expectation (which is really Christian hope) of an eternal future. To whom, then, should we look for direction? We look to Christ the Lord, who sympathizes with us in our weakness, because he also was tested and had to wait for his hour to come.

Reflective Text
Deuteronomy 4:30-41

In your distress, when all these things have happened to you in time to come, you will return to the Lord your God and heed him. Because the Lord your God is a merciful God, he will neither abandon you nor destroy you; he will not forget the covenant with your ancestors that he swore to them. For ask now about former ages, long before your own, ever since the day that God created human beings on the earth; ask from one end of heaven to the other: has anything so great as this ever happened or has its like ever been heard of? Has any people ever heard the voice of a god speaking out of a fire, as you have heard, and lived? Or has any god ever attempted to go and take a nation for himself from the midst of another nation, by trials, by signs and wonders, by war, by a mighty hand and an outstretched arm, and by terrifying displays of power, as the Lord your God did for you in Egypt before your very eyes? To you it was shown so that you would acknowledge that the Lord is God; there is no other besides him. From heaven he made you hear his voice to discipline you. On earth he showed you his great fire, while you heard his words coming out of the fire. And because he loved your ancestors, he chose their descendants after them. He brought you out of Egypt with his own presence, by his great power, driving out before you nations greater and mightier than yourselves, to bring you in, giving you their land for a possession, as it is still today. So acknowledge today and take to heart that the Lord is God in heaven above and on the earth beneath; there is no other. Keep his statutes and his commandments, which I am commanding you today for your own well-being and that of your descendants after you, so that you may long remain in the land that the Lord your God is giving you for all time.

Prayer

What powerful words, you give me, Lord God, in the voice of Moses to his people. They inspire me, even now, to look away from my present time to the land that the Lord is giving me "for all time."

That is the big leap of faith for me, God. Moving from my present time to your all time is to jump from loss to gain, from death to life, from fear to grace, from sorrow to joy. The fearful cannot jump. The foolish have no memory of your faithfulness. The blind in spirit cannot see your future with themselves happily in it. The hypochondriac fears ill health. But you, Gracious One, heal even my dejectedness. You pull me away from my need to your plenty. You turn my head to see the new age, the new life with you—Father, Son, and Holy Spirit victorious over all of our earthly enemies.

When I cannot jump and will not be pulled, you push. When I will not look, you whisper. When I will not listen and cannot hear, you open my eyes. Back and forth we go. When I deny one sense, you use another.

When I will not touch you, you touch me. When I try to forget, you remind me. When I will not try, you strengthen me. When I am too full of myself, you ask me to make room for you. When I die, you open the gate to eternal life for all time.

You are incorrigible, Jesus, bullheaded and resolute, because you know that I try to worm my way away from truth and love and sacrifice and trust. Thank you for being stronger than me, and wiser, and full of beauty. I see it. I hear it. You've touched me. Thank you. Amen

---

Reflective Questions

1. How do you define the difference between God's time and clock time?
2. According to God's time, not clock time, what time is it in your relationship with God?
3. Have you ever heard the whisper of God? What is God calling you to at this time in your life?

13

Thou Mine Inheritance

An inheritance is something precious, usually received when a loved one dies. However, we use the word more broadly, especially when we talk about our odd personalities. We might say something like, "Oh, I inherited that quirk from my mother," even though our mother is very much alive.

Inheritances can be viewed negatively. When people are born into wealth, they may be the targets of derogatory or critical comments by those who claim to disdain inheritances. Living on easy street hardly conjures up images of responsibility or a work ethic.

Jesus also indicated that inheritances have a dangerous element about them if they lead us toward the sin of greed. Here's the whole story in a couple of sentences: "Someone in the crowd said to him [Jesus], 'Teacher, tell my brother to divide the family inheritance with me.' But he said to him, 'Friend, who set me to be a judge or arbitrator over you?' And he said to them, 'Take care! Be on your guard against all kinds of greed; for one's life does not consist in the abundance of possessions'" (Luke 12:13-15).

Scripture usually views inheritance in a more positive light. Jacob's inheritance, stolen from Esau, consisted of a powerful parental blessing as well as wealth. When Job's ordeal was over and his fortunes were restored, a remarkable passage at the very end of the book states, "in all the land there were no women so beautiful as Job's daughters; and their father gave them an inheritance along with their brothers" (Job 42:15). In Hebrews, the author states that Abraham, by loving obedience to God, received an inheritance: "By faith Abraham obeyed when he was called to set out for a place that he was to receive as an inheritance; and he set out, not knowing where he was going" (Hebrews 11:8).

An inheritance is given because there is a special love relationship between the donor and the recipient, but a blood relationship is not required (see Proverbs 17:2, for example). "Family," as understood from the donor's viewpoint, is the critical criteria. Many a blood relative has been shocked to learn that being part of a will is not automatic. Being part of a family is not automatic either.

Family becomes the primary interest of persons who sense that their time is short. Old photographs and scraps from the family album are reviewed again and again. In a sense, it is the repositioning of one's whole life into the most prominent relationships given upon earth. It is looking at the whole picture of the whole life, and concluding, "This is where God put me when I was a child. Here I am in mid-life. Now this family surrounds me. This is my story."

Sometimes it's harder to receive than to give. When love has motivated us, giving has been a joy. But the time comes when we must let God have the joy of giving. We receive. It's all we can do. We have literally spent our lives. There is nothing left to give to God except a thank you. Then it's the living God's turn to give out of love to us who are dying. It's the living God's turn to remind us that we are children of God, and that we, though dying, will live. God does this through inheritance.

The word *inheritance* has in its body the sense of heritage. The legacy we receive from God at our earthly deaths is the assurance that God gives inheritances only to the living. In other words, our legacy is a new life, a new body, fit for eternal life. Our inheritance is something we will be using throughout all time to come, as living children in the family of God.

"Thou mine inheritance" is a phrase in an Irish hymn titled "Be Thou My Vision" based upon Psalm 141:8. The hymn is a prayer from beginning to an end. It has been sung in the family of God since the eighth century. All other inheritances pale in comparison to this one, for this is the receiving of eternal life from God Almighty.

Reflective Text
Psalm 141:1-2, 8

I call upon you, O Lord; come quickly to me; give ear to my voice when I call to you. Let my prayer be counted as incense before you, and the lifting up of my hands as an evening sacrifice. . . . But my eyes are turned toward you, O God, my Lord; in you I seek refuge; do not leave me defenseless.

1 Peter 1:3-9

Blessed be the God and Father of our Lord Jesus Christ! By his great mercy he has given us a new birth into a living hope through the resurrection of Jesus Christ from the dead, and into an inheritance that is imperishable, undefiled, and unfading, kept in heaven for you, who are being protected by the power of God through faith for a salvation ready to be revealed in the last time. In this you rejoice, even if now for a little while you have had to suffer various trials, so that the genuineness of your faith—being more precious than gold that, though perishable, is tested by fire—may be found to result in praise and glory and honor when Jesus Christ is revealed. Although you have not seen him, you love him; and even though you do not see him now, you believe in him and rejoice with an indescribable and glorious joy, for you are receiving the outcome of your faith, the salvation of your souls.

Prayer
Be Thou My Vision
Be thou my vision, O Lord of my heart;
Naught be all else to me, save that thou art:

Thou my best thought by day and by night,
Waking or sleeping, thy presence my light.

Be thou my wisdom, and thou my true word;
I ever with thee and thou with me, Lord.
Thou my soul's shelter, thou my high tower,
Raise thou me heav'nward, O Pow'r of my pow'r.

Riches I heed not, nor vain empty praise,
Thou mine inheritance, now and always:
Thou, and thou only, first in my heart,
Great God of heaven, my treasure thou art.

Light of my soul, after victory won,
May I reach heaven's joys, O heaven's Sun!
Heart of my own heart, whatever befall,
Still be my vision, O Ruler of all.
(*With One Voice*, 776, Irish 8th-10th cent; tr. Mary E. Byrne, 1880-1931; vers. Eleanor H. Hull, 1860-1935, alt.)

Reflective Questions

1. What have you already inherited from God?
2. How does your story read, from childhood until now?
3. When you receive the inheritance of eternal life, what do you imagine will make you smile the most?

14

Love Is Why We're Here

The philosopher in us is often nothing more than the evader of truth. As long as we can busy ourselves with tough questions about the meaning of life, we do not have to live the life of love.

Perhaps no one has made this clearer than C. S. Lewis in *The Screwtape Letters*. Wormwood, an agent of Screwtape, is in the service of Satan, and he receives advice regarding a human "patient" they wish to make a part of the kingdom of evil. In short, Wormword is accused of being naïve and is advised to guide his patient's reading, since it is well known that humans carry all sorts of conflicting philosophies and theologies in their heads. He is advised to use sound bites with his patient, and to suggest that the latest thinking is thus and so, for that is the sort of thing earthlings, like us, really care about.

As you may recall, Wormwood and Screwtape are ultimately unsuccessful in winning their patient from the loving God who lives and acts beyond philosophies. It's a fascinating, humorous journey.

Love is why we're here. This statement is not a philosophy—it is the theology of God who said through Jesus, "For God so loved the world, that he gave . . ." (John 3:16).

Love requires two qualities: the will to love and the willingness to be loved. They are equal qualities. Neither is sufficient in itself. It is often said that agape love is the highest form of love, for the giver of agape love gives without the need to receive anything, even love, in return. Agape love is described as God's love for us, for it is purely selfless.

However, it is a mistake to think that Christ, in loving us, does not desire our minds, our loyalty, our faith, and our love. If Christ does not receive such gifts from us, his love is not curtailed. We still receive grace upon grace. But Christ still yearns to hear us say, with Thomas, "My Lord and my God!" (John 20:28). God in Christ loves to be loved—even by you and me.

Receiving love from one another and from God may be far more difficult for us than giving love. Receiving makes us vulnerable. Giving makes us proud. Receiving makes us open to indebtedness. Giving makes us debt free.

God's gifts to us, when received with a grateful heart, should make us glad instead of sad. If we're sad, it's because we're focusing on our unworthiness or our need, which we'd rather not admit to. If we're glad, we've focused on the giver, God.

How many times at Christmas, during a gift opening, have you let your eyes wander away from the opener of the gift to the giver of the gift, watching, in joyful expectation, the reaction that hopefully will come from a gift well given? I've seen my own sons captivated in giving a gift to a brother, mesmerized in joy over the expected acceptance. It's a beautiful thing to witness.

When we attend the deaths of family members, our reactions may vary from uncontrollable sorrow and shock to peaceful acceptance and relief that their suffering has ended.

Earlier in these brief devotions, I related some thoughts regarding my mother's slow dying. Since writing those words she has died. My mother died almost exactly one year later than my father. Both of them were thoroughly committed Christians, and both of them died from tired, worn-out bodies.

When we received the call that my mother was near death, we hastened to her bedside. She didn't die that day, or the day after, or for several more days, to the surprise of all who were attending her. But we all knew that her time was near. After three days of not being able to communicate in any way, either by touch or sound or sight, she was in a deep sleep from which no strength was left for waking. Her body was small. Blind in one eye from a fall a few years earlier, both of her eyes were closed. Early in the morning, before sunrise, her breathing changed, and it was obvious that something was happening. I held her hand. I talked to her. I quoted Psalm 23. I named the names of all of us who loved her, one by one. There was no response. I didn't expect any.

As her last breath departed, through a strength I do not understand, she opened both eyes more widely than I had ever seen, and grinned the broadest imaginable smile, looking right past me. She spoke no word, but her countenance was radiant. What she saw, or whom she saw, I do not know. I know she was receiving a wonderful gift, an inheritance, a joy, a life—and I was watching her, seeing what I could not see or hear or touch. As Paul quoted, "What no eye has seen, nor ear heard, nor the human heart conceived, what God has prepared for those who love him" (1 Corinthians 2:9).

Reflective Text
John 14:1-6

[Jesus said,] "Do not let your hearts be troubled. Believe in God, believe also in me. In my Father's house there are many dwelling places. If it were not so, would I have told you that I go to prepare a place for you? And if I go and prepare a place for you, I will come again and will take you to myself, so that where I am, there you may be also. And you know the way to the place where I am going." Thomas said to him, "Lord, we do not know where you are going. How can we know the way?" Jesus said to him, "I am the way, and the truth, and the life. No one comes to the Father except through me."

Prayer

You claim me, Almighty God, in the name of the Father who created me, in the name of the Spirit who visits me, and in the name of the Son who died for me.

You have given everything. No saint has matched it. No poet could devise such a love. No theologian can thoroughly describe it. No pastor can preach it perfectly. No ear can hear the whole marvel.

You are beyond confession and comprehension. Earth, sea, and sky cannot contain you. Eternity is your routine experience. History is the record of your faithfulness. Time, light, and love are your hand tools. Death is no more. And I, dear God, am the object of your love and affection, made in your image, with the invisible capacities to trust, to hope, and to love.

I wait for the day of resurrection, and I look forward to the world that is coming. Give me the courage to finish the work you have assigned and, when the time is right, come, Lord Jesus, come. Amen

---

Reflective Questions

1. What are signs that we are living the life of love?
2. Who has God called you to love? Are you willing to be loved?
3. How do you feel when you receive a gift from God? What invisible capacities have you received from God?

15

Turning from Disbelief to Joy

The depths of disbelief can come upon any one of us. No matter how cheery our attitude or determined our will, disappointment and depression can lead us into the abyss of disbelief. Disbelief is beyond depression. It is more than mere confusion over God's ways. It's noting the endless silence to our prayers. No longer is it mere resentment over God's silence. It's beyond anger. It's beyond thinking, "I am an agnostic. I just don't know what God is doing, if anything."

What comes upon us in the depths is nothingness. Anger ceases, because God ceases to be present to our senses. We cannot feel God near or touch anything that is lovely. Anger dissipates, not because healing has come, but because it's hard to be angry at nothing.

The loss or losses we are experiencing make us say, "I give up because I can't change anything." Perhaps we may be able to add, "Maybe someday I'll understand. Maybe someday God will make it right." Perhaps even this is too much to hope for.

We like to be nice to God because we sense that God can zap us or our loved ones in the twinkling of an eye. But in disbelief, niceness to God doesn't matter anymore. We have taken our ball and gone home, no longer willing to play by rules that are so one-sided that victory is not in the cards. There is no capitulation from God, no mercy, and no saving from loss at the last moment.

Of course, God doesn't play this game either, because God knows this is our most desperate attempt yet to make the rules, to force God to act for us by shaming his neglect or mistreatment. But

God is after far more than our wimpy acquiescence. God is after the turning of our whole selves: body, mind, and spirit.

When God goes after our body, it means that our experience of being intensely human is about to change. When God goes after our mind, it means that our thinking has to be transformed. When God goes after our spirit, it's our soul, our personality, our will, our essence that is placed on the potter's turning wheel.

In many ways, what we face at the moment of the inevitability of death are conversions—many conversions, not just one. We are being changed, like it or not, and the more the change is resisted, the faster the potter's wheel spins. God has been planning for this renewal of our beings forever. We've been looking so hard at the pitiful lump of clay on the potter's wheel, the body that is the focus of our loss, that we have been blinded from seeing that there is a potter at work, whose name is the Lord Jesus Christ, the person who is intent upon turning us into a new creation.

Disbelief doesn't affect the Almighty at all. Christ knows how we got there, whose we are, and how faithful God has been. Nor does our agnosticism or confusion keep Christ from turning us on the potter's wheel. As far as our submission goes, it's a helpful thing, as is our acceptance of Christ. But this acceptance is a pretty lame event compared to the turning Christ is doing to us on the spinning wheel of his new creation. In other words, our acceptance is always secondary. The primary acceptance belongs to God. God says, "You are mine. I accept you. I raise you up. I resurrect you. I give you a new body, a new mind, a new soul. I do this not because you finally got your thinking straight and accepted me. I do this because you are not able to ever get your thinking straight enough, deep enough, holy enough. I turn you toward me because I love you."

True conversion is always a humiliation. Not a little humiliation, but a huge humiliation. It's not that God wants us to think of ourselves as worms. It's just the opposite. Conversion produces joy, not because of any decision we've made (we know how fickle we can be). But the realization comes that God has decided for us, and it's a decision that sticks. Though all we have is a dying body, a doubtful mind, mud that breathes but for a short while, God says, "Mine." True conversion is admitting that God does the turning by loving the unlovable, namely you, namely me, along with a host of other people we've found rather despicable during our lifetimes. We see the clay and the mud. God turns that clay and mud on the wheel, because God sees beauty.

In our pre-crisis days, we may have thought Christ to be charming or inspiring, but we had no intention of him turning our heads this far, of getting married to God. That was out of the question. The gulf was too wide. Our life experiences were incompatible. Besides, we knew we had never been particularly attractive. More to the point, God is Spirit and we are flesh. Still, the church and its members are often called "the bride of Christ." While we've been satisfied with having a relationship of respectability, admiring God's power and beauty, God has been setting love traps for us, by giving us wonderful people to call our own. While we were musing in the depths over our sorry lot, threatening God with disbelief, God placed words and wisdom into our lives beyond our grasp, and we were gripped by their power. God spoke first, taking the solemn vow that undoes disbelief because the vow is stupendously magnanimous: "I take you to be my beloved, from this day forward, for better for worse, for richer for poorer, in sickness and in health, to love and to cherish, and death will not part us."

We are speechless. We can hardly reply. We know it's our turn to make our vow, but the words seem impossible to pronounce. We are awestricken. At most all we can say is, "Oh my God!" We might only be able to nod, or to think, "yes." It is more than enough. Christ knows how irresistible he is because he is God incarnate, love incarnate, joy beyond understanding, the perfect spouse.

Christ, our partner, God incarnate, is as human as we are. We are being intensely human together, enjoying time. We are not involved in the pursuit of happiness, for joy comes as a by-product of our journey together, not as the goal of our lives. Togetherness is the goal. Through thick and thin—through pain, loss, humiliation, redemption, and resurrection—God promises that nothing shall separate us from one another.

We know that the Lord's vows will be kept, and we pray for the strength to be faithful. The old way of thinking about God with our minds and worrying about our daily lives is gone. It's not a matter of right thinking or healthy bodies after all. Those thoughts, fears, doubts, and worries kept God at a distance. We were forever trying to place God on the potter's table, pretending to be the potter of God, turning God into the right kind of God for ourselves and the world. Such nerve!

Instead, Christ walks with us toward a life that is filled with purpose and is never ending. We no longer worry about fate. We no longer think so much about ourselves, for each is giving the other all. We are part and parcel of Almighty God's world. We are under God's employment. We are making history together, in this world and the next, because we have been turned into family forever.

Disbelief, in the end, is finally unmasked for what it was from the beginning—an attempt to manipulate God into acting favorably toward us. But belief comes, as a gift, not as an accomplishment. It comes and we are surprised to find that our childhood stirrings of assurance are returning. Trust comes back, not as a leap into the dark, but as a surprising turning of our lives toward the joyous journey that is just beginning and that has no end.

Reflective Text
Jeremiah 18:1-6

The word that came to Jeremiah from the Lord: "Come, go down to the potter's house, and there I will let you hear my words." So I went down to the potter's house, and there he was working at his wheel. The vessel he was making of clay was spoiled in the potter's hand, and he reworked it into another vessel, as seemed good to him. Then the word of the Lord came to me: Can I not do with you, O house of Israel, just as this potter has done? says the Lord. Just like the clay in the potter's hand, so are you in my hand, O house of Israel.

Revelation 21:2-7

And I saw the holy city, the new Jerusalem, coming down out of heaven from God, prepared as a bride adorned for her husband. And I heard a loud voice from the throne saying, "See, the home of God is among mortals. He will dwell with them as their God; they will be his peoples, and God himself will be with them; he will wipe every tear from their eyes. Death will be no more; mourning and crying and pain will be no more, for the first things have passed away." And the one who was seated on the throne said, "See, I am making all things new." Also he said, "Write this, for these words are trustworthy and true." Then he said to me, "It is done! I am the Alpha and the Omega, the beginning and the end. To the thirsty I will give water as a gift from the spring of the water of life. Those who conquer will inherit these things, and I will be their God and they will be my children."

Prayer
Rise, Rise, Rise
Rise, rise, rise from your sleep in the earth.
Rise to new life a gift and new birth.
Rise, rise, rise, greet Redeemer, adored;
Rise, say "Good Morning," Creator, our Lord.

When the days seem too long and God's purposes weak;
Look to the day God's promised all sheep.
Fear not, have faith, God's true to the Word,
Christ shall awake us saying "Easter! Easter!"

Rise, rise, rise from your sleep in the earth.
Rise to new life a gift and new birth.
Rise, rise, rise, greet Redeemer, adored;
Rise, say "Good Morning," Creator, our Lord.

Though the tempter obscures what we know is of God,
Whispering lies, denying the Word.
Dark turns to light, Christ's Sunday shall come,
Early the morning message "Easter! Easter!"

Rise, rise, rise from your sleep in the earth.
Rise to new life a gift and new birth.
Rise, rise, rise, greet Redeemer, adored;
Rise, say "Good Morning," Creator, our Lord.

Walk the burial field with a confident stride:
Miracle place, where Christ shall arrive.
Each one shall wake to Christ's trumpet call,
Sod bursting song shall be our "Easter! Easter!"

Rise, rise, rise from your sleep in the earth.
Rise to new life a gift and new birth.
Rise, rise, rise, greet Redeemer, adored;
Rise, say "Good Morning," Creator, our Lord.

(For the music that accompanies this hymn, please go to
www.augsburgfortress.org.)

Reflective Questions

1. Have you experienced times of doubt or disbelief? What happened?
2. Have you ever been awestricken by God? What happened?
3. In what way is your natural fear of death balanced out with Christian hope?

OTHER BOOKS FROM THE LUTHERAN VOICES SERIES

Will I Sing Again? by John McCullough Bade
96 pages, 0-8066-4998-4

Author John McCullough Bade reflects on his personal struggle with Parkinson's Disease, expressing his journey in startling poetry and prose.

Listen! God Is Calling by D. Michael Bennethum
96 pages, 0-8066-4991-7

Author D. Michael Bennethum presents Martin Luther's teaching on vocation as a resource both for individual believers and for congregations. Bennethum guides readers to listen for God's call in every aspect of life.

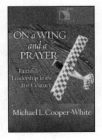

On a Wing and a Prayer by Michael L. Cooper-White
96 pages, 0-8066-4992-5

Author Michael L. Cooper-White uses the language of aviation to look at the principles of leadership and apply them to congregations and other organizations.

Let the Servant Church Arise!
by Barbara DeGrote-Sorensen and David Allen Sorensen
96 pages, 0-8066-4995-X

Authors Barbara DeGrote-Sorensen and David Allen
Sorensen explore all aspects of Christian servanthood and
how it can have a profound effect on both church and
civil communities.

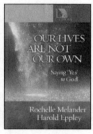

Our Lives Are Not Our Own
by Rochelle Melander and Harold Eppley
96 pages, 0-8066-4999-2

Authors Rochelle Melander and Harold Eppley
encourage personal reflective and creative dialogue
about Christian accountability for the use of our lives,
possessions, and abilities.

Reclaiming the "L" Word by Kelly A. Fryer
112 pages, 0-8066-4596-2

Inspirational, engaging, and challenging, author Kelly
A. Fryer sets forth five Guiding Principles to ignite the
church in a book that is a must-read for pastors and
congregational leaders!

Water from the Rock by Ann E. Hafften
96 pages, 0-8066-4989-5

Contributing editor Ann E. Hafften provides articles,
commentary, and stories from prominent Lutherans
living in the strife-torn land of Palestine.

Public Church by Cynthia D. Moe-Lobeda
112 pages, 0-8066-4987-9

Author Cynthia D. Moe-Lobeda explores what it means
for the ELCA to play a role in public life today. Sections
focus on what it means to be a public church, obstacles
to being a public church in public life, power for being
public church, and providing public leadership.

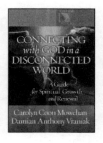

Connecting with God in a Disconnected World
by Carolyn Coon Mowchan
and Damian Anthony Vraniak.
96 pages, 0-8066-4996-8

Authors Carolyn Coon Mowchan and Damian
Anthony Vraniak encourage adult readers to examine
the barriers that keep us from experiencing a more full
relationship with God.

Give Us This Day by Craig L. Nessan
96 pages, 0-8066-4993-3

Author Craig L. Nessan summons the Christian
church to listen to the cries of the hungry and commit
itself to ending hunger as a matter of *status confessionis*.